Tudor and Stuart Texts

The True Law of Free Monarchies
and
Basilikon Doron

Tudor and Stuart Texts

Series editors

DAVID GALBRAITH
Department of English, University of Toronto

GERMAINE WARKENTIN
Department of English, University of Toronto

This is a series of modernized scholarly editions of important English Renaissance and Reformation texts, published by the Centre for Reformation and Renaissance Studies. The series emphasizes texts which have not been produced in modern editions and whose availability will contribute to ongoing attempts to interpret and to teach the English Renaissance.

Titles published

The True Law of Free Monarchies and *Basilikon Doron*
JAMES I. Ed. Daniel Fischlin and Mark Fortier

For a list of CRRS publications see page 183.

James I

The True Law
of
Free Monarchies
and
Basilikon Doron

A modernized edition

Edited, with an Introduction by
Daniel Fischlin
and Mark Fortier

Toronto
Centre for Reformation and Renaissance Studies
1996

CRRS Publications
Centre for Reformation and Renaissance Studies
Victoria University in the University of Toronto
Toronto, Canada M5S 1K7

Canadian Cataloguing in Publication Data

James I, King of England, 1566–1625
    The true law of free monarchies ; and, Basilikon
doron

(Tudor and Stuart texts)
A modernized ed.
Includes bibliographical references.
ISBN 0-9697512-6-5

1. Monarchy. 2. Divine rights of kings. 3. Education
of princes. 4. Kings and rulers – Duties. I. Fischlin,
Daniel Thomas, 1957–   II. Fortier, Mark, 1953–
III. Victoria University (Toronto, Ont.). Centre for
Reformation and Renaissance Studies. IV. Title.
V. Title: Basilikon doron. VI. Series.

JC153.J3 1996   321'.6   C96-931326-8

for
Zoé, Hannah, & Martha
&
Faye, Charlotte, & Julia

Contents

List of Illustrations

Acknowledgements

This text could not have been produced without the judicious guidance of both David Galbraith and Germaine Warkentin, general editors of the CRRS Tudor and Stuart Texts series. Many people have contributed to the long and difficult process of assembling information. Lisa Guenther provided crucial help as a research assistant; Robert Spencer made a generous offer of illustrations from his private collection of Elizabethan and Jacobean books; Stephen Greenblatt, Jonathan Goldberg, and Ian Sowton made helpful interventions at early stages of the project; Dr. Louise Yeoman of the Scottish National Library and Geoffrey Barré of *The Word* bookstore in Montreal gave of their time and expertise in helping with a number of troublesome annotations; Faye Pickrem undertook essential research and compiled the glossary; the students in the honours seminar "Poetics and Politics in Elizabethan and Jacobean England," all of whom read and commented on an initial draft of this text, were particularly helpful in their critiques; Jenny Wormald, of St. Hilda's College, Oxford, was generous of her time and expertise, and we owe her a large debt of gratitude for her commentary; the anonymous readers for the CRRS made constructive suggestions that helped shape the final version of this edition; a number of libraries provided their facilities for research, including the Robarts Library of the University of Toronto, the E. J. Pratt Library at Victoria College, the special collection of the Centre for Reformation and Renaissance Studies (Victoria University), the McLennan Library (McGill University), the Dartmouth Library Special Collections, the British Library, the Bodleian Library (Oxford), the National Library of Scotland, the Edinburgh University Library, and the University of Strathclyde Library; research and writing were aided by a grant from the University of Toronto and another from the English Department at the University of Toronto; David Bevan, vice-principal responsible for academic research at Bishop's University, provided much needed funding and letters of support; the significant financial support of the University of Guelph Research Board as well as the institutional support proffered by Wayne C. Marsh, Director of Research Services, Carole Stewart, Dean of the College of Arts, and Gerald Manning, Chair of the Department of English, made the completion of this project possible—their support is gratefully acknowledged; finally, this work would not have been feasible without the pioneering efforts of the Scottish scholar James Craigie, to whom we owe special recognition for having done much of the laborious investigative work upon which our own work stands. We can only hope that this volume in some small measure lives up to the exacting standards set by Professor Craigie.

James VI and I and the Literature of Kingship

The writings of James VI and I, especially *The True Law of Free Monarchies* (1598) and *Basilikon Doron* (1599)—but also *Dæmonologie*, sundry speeches to the English Parliament, and a substantial body of poetry—are more often known of than known and read. This is in large measure because they are not available in adequately annotated and modernized editions. The present volume is an attempt to begin to rectify this situation. Once a reader engages with these texts, he or she will find that they are of interest on any number of counts. The product of a unique historical personage—as Jenny Wormald states, "[n]ot since Alfred had a ruler combined the practice and the theory of kingship in his own person" (Peck 36)—they shed considerable light on the mind and personality of power in early modern Scotland and England. *The True Law* and *Basilikon Doron*, moreover, are not merely historical curiosities or amateur diversions, but political discourses rich in points of rhetorical procedure as well as content. Both are significant sixteenth-century texts, not only for what they reveal about the literature of Renaissance kingship but also for the wide range of their intertextual influence.

In distinction from *The True Law of Free Monarchies*, a theoretical justification of the divine right of kings, *Basilikon Doron* (or the king's gift) may be understood as a pragmatic guide, a "how to" book, that distills James's personal experiences as king of Scotland, with his scholarly and (some might say) literary notions of the ideal comportment of the monarch. The former addresses a generalized (and public) audience of sceptics regarding James's hereditary right to the English throne using a metaphysical argument based on Scriptural sources; the latter is, ostensibly, a private address to James's first-born son, Henry, using the vast body of classical and contemporary referents that James had at his command to delimit monarchic conduct in everything from choice of clothing to conjugal relations to knowledge of the liberal arts. Both texts, it must be remembered, were born of the Scottish experience of kingship, and embody a deep knowledge of the European debate on the power and legitimising authority of kingship; both were written by a Scottish sovereign—James VI, not James I—but with an eye to the English throne.

Our rationale for selecting these two texts as significant representatives of James's political thinking is simple. *Basilikon Doron* constitutes an odd hybrid of private and public performativity on the part of James, the first edition being intended, as much as such intentions are ever knowable, only for private familial consumption, later editions (1603 and after) being intended for public consumption. For this reason it marks an intersection in the play between public and private notions of the political from the absolute monarch's point of view, while also marking the shift in political philosophy (if such a shift may be delineated) that occurs with James's transition from James VI of Scotland to James I of England. *The True Law of Free Monarchies*, on the other hand, represents a considered public performance that overtly theorizes the "reciprocal and mutual duties between a free king and his natural subjects" and for this reason constitutes a clear and concise pronunciation on the relationship between ruled and ruler formulated from the point of view of the latter.

The two texts, taken together, exemplify many of the contradictions that arise out of the exercise of absolute power in the Scottish and English Renaissance, not the least of which are the political anxieties that, paradoxically, arise for the absolute monarch from within a position that constructs the fiction of an absolute power. The chronic challenges to James from the Scottish kirk, from the English Parliament, from various members of the nobility, all demonstrate the precarious nature of an absolutism more imagined than real. Both *The True Law* and *Basilikon Doron* have important things to say about how power is exercised and constructed through imaginative acts of textual representation, the literature of kingship. Both texts demonstrate James's singular skill in the manipulation of the complex legal, theological, and literary referents that give substance and shape to his political will.

Susanne Collier has noted that "[c]riticism of James's literary output is surprisingly limited; indeed, except for the interest of new historicist critics in the political concerns of Renaissance literature, specific

James VI and I, engraving by Simon Pass. Frontispiece to *The Workes of … James* (1616). Reproduced by courtesy of Robert Spencer.

discussion of James's writings is largely confined to regarding him as a possible source for Jacobean plays" (515). Such a view may be distinguished from comments made by James Craigie, whose work laid the foundations for much subsequent James scholarship: "[h]ad [James] used his native literary gifts on subjects in which later generations could find more of interest than they do, his reputation as a writer would have stood much higher than it is usually placed" (*Basilikon Doron* 2.62). Craigie understood that as the subject matter of literary inquiry shifted, so too would James's literary reputation. Furthermore, Craigie viewed *The True Law of Free Monarchies* and *Basilikon Doron* as "complementary to each other," arguing that they "should be regarded as the two halves of a single work" (*Basilikon Doron* 2.76). Whether or not such an observation is entirely accurate, it is clear that these two texts have an intertextual relationship to each other evident at both the political and literary levels.

The historian Maurice Lee Jr.'s position is that while *The True Law of Free Monarchies* and *Basilikon Doron* represent "James's prose at its very best .... [t]hey have both been analyzed to death, from every conceivable point of view, and it would take a brave scholar indeed to assert that there was something new to say about their contents" (*Great Britain's Solomon* 63–64). Rather than discounting James's literary work, Lee seems to dismiss the possibility of new critical insight into James's output, a position directly at odds with Collier's assessment of recent James criticism cited above. And yet, Lee himself argues, somewhat contradictorily, that both texts are worth "reconsideration because, taken together, they reveal James's beliefs about the business of being a king in late sixteenth-century Scotland, beliefs he took with him when he moved to his greater kingdom in 1603" (64). More specifically, Jennifer M. Brown[1] has argued that the two texts "introduced ... a concept of monarchy which was totally new to Scotland, based on the theory that kings were answerable to God alone and not to their people" (22), James's intent being to end "the long struggle for control by the monarchy over a nobility which had for at least two centuries enjoyed too much power" (22). Wormald provides yet another perspective on this position, arguing that "the political issue which concerned [James] most when he

---

[1]Note that Jenny Wormald and Jennifer M. Brown are the same person, the latter being the name under which Wormald published her early work.

succeeded to the English throne was not divine right monarchy at all, but union" (Peck 53). Whether from an historical, political, or literary perspective, then, it is clear that *The True Law of Free Monarchies* and *Basilikon Doron* are seminal works in which historical contingency, political will, and literary style come together in a compelling manner.

The shifting grounds of textual studies in literary theory, English and comparative literature, history, political science, cultural studies, and so forth, provide a unique opportunity to reconsider James's literary and historical context as both an early modern writer and monarch. The texts chosen for modernization in this edition represent significant elements in James's political and literary constructions of kingship during a critical period prior to his ascension to the English throne. For James, textuality was perhaps as much a means to the end of power as was direct political action. James recognized textual representation as crucial to the construction of both the political subject and the sovereign, whose power depended on creating such a subject. The representation of power by literary means, in such a context, was a substantial element in constituting both the self-identity and the public identity of the sovereign.

For James, the plausibility of the divine right of kingship and of absolutism as political principles in which he had more than a vested interest, depended, in part, on the textual relations between the sovereign as author and his political subjects as readers. In this last regard, the authorial construction of a reader's experience may be seen as analogous to the state's construction of political subjectivity. If for no other reason, readers in various disciplines will find James's key political works of more than passing interest because they embody a specific early modern notion of kingship, one heavily dependent upon techniques of textual self-representation. Without understanding the importance of textual representation as a means of fashioning early modern notions of power, it seems inconceivable that an appropriate grasp of the wide range of literary genres written during that period—a period, moreover, in which kingship figures as a crucial trope—can be attained. In short, though scholarship has afforded James's texts a modest renown, it has not made them any more accessible to students and teachers of the Renaissance—and this in a pedagogical climate that, at the very least, requires careful attention to primary texts in a classroom situation. This CRRS edition of James's key political works seeks to remedy that situation.

Biographical Sketch

On August 15, 1584, M. de Fontenay, then envoy of Mary Stuart, sent a report to Mary's secretary that contains a surprisingly detailed description, however accurate, of the then eighteen-year-old king:

> Three qualities of the mind he possesses in perfection: he understands clearly, judges wisely, and has a retentive memory. His questions are keen and penetrating and his replies are sound. In any argument, whatever it is about, he maintains the view that appears to him most just, and I have heard him support Catholic against Protestant opinions. He is well-instructed in languages, science, and affairs of state, better, I dare say, than anyone else in his kingdom. In short, he has a remarkable intelligence, as well as lofty and virtuous ideals and a high opinion of himself .... He dislikes dancing and music, and the little affectations of courtly life such as amorous discourse or curiosities of dress, and has a special aversion for ear-rings. In speaking and eating, in his dress and in his sports, in his conversation in the presence of women, his manners are crude and uncivil and display a lack of proper instruction. He is never still in one place but walks constantly up and down, though his gait is erratic and wandering, and he tramps about even in his own chamber. His voice is loud and his words grave and sententious. He loves the chase above all other pleasures and will hunt for six hours without interruption, galloping over hill and dale with loosened bridle. His body is feeble and yet he is not delicate. In a word, he is an old young man.
>
> I have remarked in him three defects that may prove injurious to his estate and government: he does not estimate correctly his poverty and insignificance but is over-confident of his strength and scornful of other princes; his love for favourites is indiscreet and wilful and takes no account of the wishes of his people; he is too lazy and indifferent about affairs, too given to pleasure, allowing all business to be conducted by others. Such things are excusable at his age, yet I fear they may become habitual. (Willson 53)

Sir Anthon Weldon, who was knighted by James in 1617 and who became a particularly aggressive critic of the Stuarts, characterized the older James as "crafty and cunning in petty things, as the circumventing any great man, the change of a favourite etc., insomuch as a very wise man was wont to say he believed him the wisest fool in Christendom, meaning him wise in small things, but a fool in weighty affairs" (Houston 113–14). Weldon, who fell from James's favour after having written a nasty satire of Scottish manners, painted a less than flattering portrait of James, whose reportedly overlarge tongue and strange "circular" walk in which he fiddled with his cod-piece became damning physical descriptions that pandered to anti-royalist propagandists.

Both descriptions have done much to stereotype James as an effete, or worse, a fool. Yet James produced an enormous body of writing on matters political and literary, and survived years of political instability in Scotland before acceding to the throne of England, where he enjoyed a substantial period of relative political stability. The minor cult of personality surrounding James has all too often relied on such details as his love of favourites, his tendency to impecuniousness, his putative Scottish backwardness, the decadence of his court, and his love of the hunt, to portray a man who was considerably more complicated and interesting than such trite portraits would suggest. Part of the reason for this portrayal is a certain Anglocentric vision of James as the unsophisticated and inept Scotsman who by hereditary fluke happened to become king of England. The problem with such a view, however, is the degree to which it misrepresents the complex concatenation of events that led to James's accession to both the Scottish and English thrones, not to mention the immensely rich and varied cultural context that fed into the making of James as a political and literary figure of historical consequence.

Some of the events with the greatest influence on James's life happened long before he was born. Perhaps none was more important than the marriage in 1503 of James IV, king of Scotland, and Margaret Tudor, daughter and sister, respectively, of Henry VII and Henry VIII, kings of England. From his great grandfather, James inherited the crown of Scotland; however, because the children of Henry VIII had no children of their own, James inherited from his great grandmother an even more potent claim: throughout the final years of the sixteenth century he knew that upon the death of Elizabeth I he would be, at least by birthright, the foremost claimant to the throne of England. In his time as king of Scotland, James prized the English crown, and especially as the sixteenth century waned, no other goal preoccupied him more. There were obstacles, however, to his claim: English law did not allow a foreigner to ascend the throne; Henry VIII's will had disinherited Margaret Tudor and her descendants. These obstacles were formidable, and because of them James suffered much anxiety and uncertainty. Because of them, perhaps, James also invested much of his intellectual and polemical energy in the defense of the hereditary rights of kings.

James's place in the Scottish succession was also marked by events before his birth, as well as events in his infancy. His mother, Mary Queen of Scots, was first married to François II, king of France, but François died in 1560, before there were any children born to the marriage. Mary then married Henry Stuart, Lord Darnley, in 1565. James was born to Mary and Darnley in 1566. The marriage was a troubled one and in 1567 Darnley was murdered, perhaps with Mary's approval or participation. She quickly married James Hepburn, Earl of Bothwell, in 1567. This marriage brought upon her widespread outrage and disapproval, and Mary was deposed in 1567 and replaced on the throne by her infant son. The subsequent civil war lasted until 1573. James's early years were lived under a series of regents who controlled him, and were punctuated by traumatic periods of danger and upheaval, most notably the Ruthven raid of 1582, in which James was kidnapped by the earls of Gowrie, Mar, and Glencairn in the hope of seizing power and influence over him. Because of, or in spite of, this early turmoil, James grew into a staunch defender of royal absolutism and by the last decade of the sixteenth century was more or less in control of the Scottish state.

Mary's reign had been marked by opposition from the reformed Scottish church, or kirk. Most notable was the clash between Mary and the Protestant reformer John Knox upon her return from France in 1561. Much of this opposition had to do with Mary's Catholicism. Throughout his life, James professed his Protestant beliefs; however, his religious views, especially his views on church hierarchy (and subsequently his views on political hierarchy), remained at odds with those of the religious reformers. Consequently, James spent his time in Scotland in repeated confrontations with the kirk, most notably with Andrew Melville, the reform clergyman, in 1596 and 1597, just before the composition of *The True Law of Free Monarchies* and *Basilikon Doron*. James's struggles with religious leaders who argued for limitations to his royal prerogative are one of the foremost concerns of his period as king of Scotland.

The kirk's view of limited monarchical power was echoed by James's tutor, the prominent radical historian and political philosopher George Buchanan, who was in charge of James's instruction until he reached the age of fourteen. Buchanan held the view that there were, philosophically and historically, a number of legitimate checks to royal power. In adulthood James thoroughly rejected Buchanan's views, although many of his own arguments are—if in opposition—dictated by Buchanan's agenda.

In 1587 James had to deal with the tricky business of his mother's execution in England on charges of conspiracy to assassinate Elizabeth. Although he had been an infant at the time, his coming to the throne of Scotland had been at his mother's expense; however, it was necessary, as son or politician, for him to express opposition to his mother's death. More importantly, it was necessary that he not offend Elizabeth in any way that would jeopardize her support of his claim to the English crown. That this was a delicate situation can be seen in the way that, years later, a misunderstanding on this point (people in England took James's remark equating loyalty to his mother with loyalty to himself as a veiled threat) is one of the main reasons for James's revision of *Basilikon Doron,* on the verge of his ascendance to the throne of England in 1603.

In 1589 James had to deal with another crisis, this time the conspiracies of Francis Stewart, Earl of Bothwell, who was reported to have used witchcraft against James. Bothwell, fearing arrest, escaped to England and returned in 1591 in an attempt to overthrow the king. James was unsettled by these events, but Bothwell's attempts ultimately failed and he fled to Italy.

James married Anne, princess of Denmark, in 1589, and in 1594 she gave birth to their first son, Henry (d. 1612). James, the kingdom of Scotland, and, later, England invested much hope in Henry's future. Possibly fearing his own early death, James wrote *Basilikon Doron* for Henry's instruction. The implicit hope was that if he himself never attained the English crown, his son would. Moreover, should James die, Henry would be adequately prepared to implement his father's political agenda by the detailed advice proffered him in the text. *Basilikon Doron* was, as Jonathan Goldberg has persuasively argued, a form of proleptic control of the future, the text "binding the prince to [James], even as [James] assures [Henry] of his unaccountability to the populace" (119). It was not James, however, who was to die prematurely.

The True Law and *Basilikon Doron,* then, were both written in 1598 or 1599, after James had secured his authority in Scotland and was awaiting Elizabeth's passing. His earlier writings include two books of poetry, *The Essayes of a Prentise, in the Divine Art of Poesie* (1584) and *His Maiesties Poeticall Exercises at Vacant Houres* (1591), and the infamous treatise on witchcraft, *Dæmonologie* (1597). Throughout his life James had an active and varied scholarly and authorial career. His interests and writings ranged widely: from biblical exegesis, exemplified in "A Paraphrase upon the Revelation of the Apostle S. John" and "A Meditation upon the Lords Prayer," to biblical translation, which he actively supported through the production of the Authorized Version of the Bible (1611), to his translation of the French Huguenot poet Du Bartas' *L'Uranie* and *Les Furies,* to a long historical poem based on the battle of Lepanto, to a prescient anti-smoking treatise entitled "A Counterblaste to Tobacco," in which he ends with the memorable line calling tobacco smoking "a custom loathsome to the eye, hateful to the nose, harmful to the brain, dangerous to the lungs, and in the black stinking fume thereof, nearest resembling the horrible Stygian smoke of the pit that is bottomless" (*Workes* 222). In addition James produced numerous political treatises that elaborate a sophisticated notion of kingship and the exercise of monarchic power. These treatises, to list a few, include "A Defence of the Right of Kings," "To all Christian Monarches, Free Princes and States," "An Apologie for the Oath of Allegiance," and "A Paterne for a Kings Inauguration." The body of his literary output, then, is impressive and substantial—not the work of a literary dilettante or epigone, but the work of a serious writer and scholar with a developed voice and a number of original things to say on a variety of topics.

In this latter regard, *The True Law* is a theoretical defense of the hereditary and absolute rights of kingship—an answer to both those like Buchanan and some in the kirk who argued for the limitation of royal power and those in England who would bar him from the throne. *Basilikon Doron* is a book of advice to his young son. It was originally printed privately in 1599 in an edition of only seven copies. Somehow, however, the book got into the hands of James's opponents, including Melville, who used James's arguments, sometimes distorted, to attack him. James revised the book to clarify or alter certain contentious points (such as his views on so-called "Puritans"), and editions of the revised text were published in Edinburgh and London in early 1603, as Elizabeth's health was rapidly failing. With its author positioned to take up the English throne, *Basilikon Doron* was translated into most of the languages of Europe and became an international bestseller.

When Elizabeth died, James, as he had always hoped, succeeded her as the English monarch. In England James encountered a church hierarchy which, having made the break from Catholicism with its bishops and archbishops intact, was more to his liking; but he also encountered a degree of parliamentary independence of mind for which nothing in Scotland had prepared him. His first major defeat occurred over his plans to bring together his two kingdoms in an act of union. From 1604 to 1607 Parliament struggled with him over this plan, and James was forced to concede defeat. Bruce Galloway has argued that "James's plans [for union] were notably successful, outside parliament" (167): "Besides union in outward marks of government and pacification of the Borders, James was able to secure permanent naturalisation of the *Post-Nati* [people born after March 24, 1603, the day Elizabeth died, who were considered to be legal citizens in either kingdom], abolition of hostile laws, the establishment of common law judicial arrangements in the 'Middle Shires,' and several years of free trade between the nations" (167). Nonetheless, these putative successes aside, the union of England and Scotland was not to be enacted by Parliament until 100 years later, in 1707. Throughout the rest of his reign James found himself at odds with his Parliament. James's struggles with Parliament affected the writings of his English period: while the writings of the Scottish period are largely concerned with opposition from the kirk, after 1603 James's work is dominated by a series of speeches (1603, 1605, 1607, 1609) to Parliament on the nature and extent of royal prerogative.

In 1612 Prince Henry, who had become a celebrated and dashing national icon, died an untimely death at age 18 of typhoid fever. Henry's death prompted an outpouring of grief, exemplified in *Songs of Mourning* (1613), a song cycle with lyrics by Thomas Campion and music by John Coprario. The penultimate song, "When Pale Famine," addressed "To the most disconsolate Great Britain," suggests that "Now thy highest States lament a son and brother's loss ... Thy commons are with passion sad, to think how brave a prince they had" (32–33). In any event, the expectations lavished on Henry now fell upon his younger and less imposing brother, Charles. When James's collected *Workes* were published in 1616, they were dedicated, in an opening epistle by the Bishop of Winchester, to the new heir apparent. In this new context—of English Parliaments, death, and the revision of legacies and expectations—*The True Law* and especially *Basilikon Doron* took on a changed significance.

James died on Sunday, March 27, 1625 at the age of 59, after having caught a "tertian ague" that led to a collapse, possibly from a stroke. The Venetian ambassador, writing in April, suggested that James "did not know his disease, which grew worse and became very serious ... when he had an apoplectic fit, which affected his chin, loosening his jawbone and enlarging his tongue, and finally a violent dysentry carried him off" (Bergeron 185). Ironically, the man who had invested such energy in the power of the word "ended his days speechless" (Fraser 209).

The True Law of Free Monarchies

Although the theory of "the divine right of kings" arose in sixteenth-century France in the face of intellectual and political attempts to limit royal authority, a number of the key figures, on both sides, were Scots with substantial French connections: on the one side, George Buchanan; on the other, William Barclay, who published the encyclopedic *De Regno et Regali Potestate (On Kingship and Royal Power)* in Paris in 1608, and James himself.

Buchanan was a central intellectual force in the arguments against unlimited royal prerogative. As James's tutor, he dedicated his treatise of 1579, *De Jure Regni apud Scotos (The Powers of the Crown in Scotland),* to his young pupil (Buchanan's dedicatory letter to James sets up the treatise as a guide much as James himself was later to do for his son Henry with *Basilikon Doron).* James appears to have been made to read the treatise fairly carefully. *The True Law of Free Monarchies,* James's foremost discussion of royal prerogative, is profoundly influenced in a great many of its details by Buchanan's work. Craigie, in his introduction to *The True Law (Minor Prose* 193–197), downplays the connections between these two works. He argues that James wrote because of a series of provocations and threatening incidents involving Andrew Melville and others; he refers, for instance, to the incident in 1596 when Melville took the king by the sleeve and called him "God's sillie vassall." Much of the energy of *The True Law* is directed against the kirk; yet even if such events were the emotional source of James's need to write *The True Law,* they hardly explain the particulars of James's arguments. Here Craigie severely underemphasizes the connections between Buchanan's arguments and James's refutations; in our footnotes we have noted a number of places where James's discussion echoes Buchanan's. Craigie also argues that, since Buchanan's work had already been officially condemned by the Scottish Parliament, there was no further need to answer it. Buchanan's work, however, continued to be pivotal, influential, and startling long after the end of the sixteenth century (Allen 342). At any rate, *The Powers of the Crown in Scotland* may serve as the foremost example of the arguments James attacks in the particulars of *The True Law.*

Opinions of *The True Law* as a work of political philosophy have varied widely. Early in the twentieth century, John Neville Figgis and J. W. Allen took opposed positions: for Figgis it contains "the doctrine of Divine Right complete in every detail" (138); Allen found it impossible to extract from James's work any distinct theory of kingship or the state (252). Later Charles McIlwain found it "the most comprehensive of all [James's] political writings" (xxxvii), while Wilfrid Harrison doubted "to what extent a significant doctrine of the divine right of kings is to be found in King James's not too coherent book" (31). Few extended discussions of *The True Law* have been written; however, Sabine and Thorson dedicate more space to James than to any other writer in their discussion of divine right (367–369).

Recent scholarly discussion has questioned the significance and importance of James's belief in divine right or absolute monarchical authority. In "James I and the Divine Right of Kings," J. P. Sommerville argues that there was no consensus around issues of political authority in England, that James's continentalist ideas set him at true odds with English common law theorists, and that James attempted to put his ideas into practice, which explains his conflicts with the English Parliament. Wormald, however, qualifies James's views on divine right by stressing the "reciprock" nature of the duties and responsibilities between monarch and people. Glenn Burgess argues that the idea of divine right was in no way controversial as long as it was aligned with an adherence to common law principles, and James's theory and practice were not a challenge to the common law. Thus readers of *The True Law* looking for a simple explication of the doctrine of divine right should understand that James's notions on the subject are complicated and perhaps ambiguous.

What is lacking is an extended discussion of *The True Law* as political discourse. In *Politics and Ideas in Early Stuart England*, Kevin Sharpe calls for a fuller "understanding of the relationship of ideas, values and styles to politics and the exercise of power" (xi). Using ideas from Sharpe's discussion, one can understand the way *The True Law* relies upon common discursive practices of the period: the use of biblical citation as an endorsement of a position; argument by analogy; the reliance upon the commonplaces of fatherly authority and the rule of the head over the body; the resort to classical precedent. What is most characteristic of James's treatise is its juxtaposition of very different bases of argumentation. Beginning with a biblical exegesis, which for James of itself clinches his argument, the text moves from historical precedent, to argument by analogy, and finally, to the answering of specific objections that entail questions on the nature of law, divine justice, and the dubious advisability of rebellion and social disorder. If James's arguments hang together, they hang together in a specifically early modern way—by heterogeneous addition; they do not proceed by the scientistic principles of unity and logical consistency that have been so favoured since the Enlightenment.

Sharpe draws connections and contrasts between political tracts and early modern theatre (22–23). Here he follows upon Goldberg's groundbreaking *James I and the Politics of Literature,* which makes connections between James's political and textual practices and the response to James in the works of such writers as Donne, Jonson, and Shakespeare. James was, of course, the most prominent person in early Stuart England; his works did not go unnoticed. There is much work still to be done in drawing the polemical connections between James's work and the literary work of the period. To point the way to this discussion, we have included a number of footnotes that draw connections between James's texts and works by Shakespeare.

Despite any incoherence in James's theoretical principles, despite uncertainties as to how James's thought fits into the beliefs and practices of his time, and despite the heterogeneous grounds of his argumentation, *The True Law* is a deeply partisan and one-sided work. It has an overwhelmingly unified sense of purpose: to argue for *the* true law, single and unassailably right, which supports James's sense of his own kingly authority. Certainly James is capable of taking up arguments opposed to his own, but there is not in James's work an ability to take up equally either side of an argument such as Joel Altman traces in *The Tudor Play of Mind.* Neither is there, when James submits that "wrong might be admitted in play," anything like the potentially open and interrogative dramatization of different perspectives to be found in some early modern English drama. *The True Law* is through and through an authoritarian text: free monarchy entails setting limits on argumentative free play.

Basilikon Doron

In 1599, while James was still king of Scotland, and with Elizabeth's death still four years distant, pamphlets were distributed that objected to James's title to the English throne. In response,

James employed some learned men in his kingdom to answer to these cavillers, and to explain the advantages which would result to both kingdoms, by the union of the Crowns. These books were eagerly read, and contributed not a little to reconcile the English to that event. A book published this year, by the King himself, produced an effect still more favourable. It was intitled *Basilicon Doron,* and contained precepts concerning the art of government, addressed to Prince Henry his son. Notwithstanding the great alterations and refinements in national taste since that time, we must allow this to be no contemptible performance, and not to be inferior to the works of most contemporary writers, either in purity of style or justness of composition. Even the vain parade of erudition with which it abounds, and which now disgusts us, raised the admiration of that age; and it was filled with those general rules, which speculative authors deliver for rendering a nation happy, and of which James could discourse with great plausibility, though often incapable of putting them in practice; the English conceived an high opinion of his abilities, and expected an increase of national honour and prosperity, under a Prince so profoundly skilled in politics, and who gave such a specimen both of his wisdom, and of his love to his people. (Robertson 2.245–46)

The passage, from the eighteenth-century historian William Robertson, firmly establishes the contexts in which *Basilikon Doron* may be read as an epideictic text, meant to demonstrate political skill, scholarly wisdom, and concern for the commonweal. It is clearly a performative text that had its value in assuaging English suspicions regarding James's ability to rule and, in William Robertson's reading, it exemplifies how the actual practice of James's politics was so often detached from its idealized and imaginary foundations. One of the distinguishing features of *Basilikon Doron* in its relation to James's other writings, then, is that it marks, as we have earlier suggested, the intersection between private and public notions of monarchic self-representation. Its complicated publishing history suggests that the first edition (Robert Waldegrave, 1599) was intended for a limited audience (only seven copies were printed) of family and nobility including Anne of Denmark, James's wife, his eldest son Henry, and the earls of Huntly, Erroll, and Angus, the latter three being people, oddly enough, "who had had a long run of defiance of the [Scottish] Crown in the late 1580s and early 1590s" (Brown 22).

Basilikon Doron's putative private context was that of the wise father offering advice and *bons mots* as a personal testimonial and legacy to his son. The fact, however, that the royal holograph was in

Scots, but the first limited edition was in English, may suggest that James had bigger plans for the book, especially in terms of demonstrating his competence as a ruler to a suspicious English public. Whatever James's intentions, *Basilikon Doron* seems to have mutated from a text that was meant to have a rather limited circulation to a text that embodied central tenets of James's monarchic ethos for a public audience needing to be convinced regarding his leadership. Thus, there is a subtle distinction to be drawn between *Basilikon Doron* and James's other writings, including *The True Law of Free Monarchies, Dæmonologie,* and various speeches, which were clearly intended to have a more obviously public context.

The mystery and secrecy surrounding *Basilikon Doron's* genesis and early publishing history would suggest that it had the added allure, once it reached a wider public, of representing, however fictively, the immensely attractive spectacle of the king's private self. This was not an insignificant consideration for a wily politician like James, who understood the need for personal myth-making. Such a need would have been especially significant in the context of displacing the potent personal myths surrounding Elizabeth I, whose putative virginity was a significant element in a complex system of personal representation that Elizabeth had evolved to help her achieve political ends. These, then, are but some of the political reasons that may be attributed to James in his writing of *Basilikon Doron.*

Craigie notes another more personal (and perhaps apocryphal) reason suggested by George Nicolson, the English agent at the Scottish court at the time of *Basilikon Doron's* writing, sometime in the summer or fall of 1598. In a letter to Sir William Cecil, Lord Burghley, one of Elizabeth's key advisors, in which the ciphers .126 and .200 were used to denote James and Elizabeth, respectively, Nicolson suggested that

> .126 was troubled in his chamber in his sleep. And has taken conceipt that .200 shall outlive him. And thereon has written an apology and rule how his son shall be brought to succeed .200 to that place [the English throne], and how all shall be governed for the attaining thereunto ... (*Basilikon Doron* 2.4; modernized)

Though Henry was but four years old at the time, it is clear that James had a great deal invested in his own or his son's ascension to the English throne. Whether true or not, the account creates an appropriately literary context for the writing of *Basilikon Doron* as an enactment of oneiric vision brought about by political and personal anxiety. It is useful to note that shortly after Elizabeth's death at two or three in the morning of March 24, 1603, printing presses in London began reprinting *Basilikon Doron,* copies of which were available by March 28—an indication of the degree to which it embodied the values and aspirations of James's dream of political union with England, not to mention the idealized image of sovereignty that he sought to convey to the English public.

In order to convey this idealized image, James composed *Basilikon Doron* as a learned synthesis, a composite portrait, of commonplaces regarding kingship and statecraft, taken from numerous classical, medieval, and biblical sources that provide similar advice on kingship, statecraft, and political theory. These sources range from Plato and Aristotle to Cicero, Quintilian, Isocrates, Xenophon, Plutarch, Thucydides, Geoffrey of Monmouth, and so forth. A partial listing of these sources would include Plato's *Republic* and *Laws,* Aristotle's *Politics* and *Ethics,* Plutarch's *The Lives of the Noble Grecians and Romans,* Cicero's *De Legibus, De Finibus,* and *De Officiis (On Laws, On [the different conceptions of] the Chief Good and Evil,* and *On Duties),* Seneca's *Moral Essays,* and the historical works of Livy and Tacitus. Not only does *Basilikon Doron* provide a remarkable compendium of the received knowledge and attitudes— political, philosophical, moral, theological—of the time, it also provides a detailed rendering of the kinds of information deemed significant to a ruler-in-waiting that is, significantly, derived from a long literary tradition of such writings. For James to have written such a work would have been in keeping with his characteristic fondness for "literary discourse" (cited in Willson 136), as described by Sir Henry Wotton, an English diplomat and poet who met James in Scotland in 1601. *Basilikon Doron* is thus both a proleptic rendering of what young Henry would be expected to know in acceding to power and a literary accounting of James's experiences as sovereign. Part of its significance, then, lies in its didactic depiction of ethical behaviour that accounts for the particular expectations, both private and public, that devolve upon the figure of the king.

While *The True Law* is structured as a series of overlapping arguments, *Basilikon Doron,* like Francis Bacon's *Essays* (1596), consists of aphoristic precepts—fleshed out with much erudition and observation. Perhaps nothing makes this quality of *Basilikon Doron* clearer than the emblem book that Henry Peacham made from James's text. The two versions of Peacham's book, now in the British

Library (Royal MS 12 A lxvi and Harley MS 6855 Art. 13), one dedicated to Henry, the other to James, reconstitute James's prose as a series of discrete emblematic sayings, 79 in one instance, 65 in the other. Each saying is accompanied by an emblematic image, a four line Latin verse, and quotations from classical and, much less often, biblical analogues. In light of Peacham's book, it is not just generalizations and truisms that are emblematic, but pressing and current religious and political concerns. There is an emblem, for instance, that accompanies James's assertion in the second book that there is more pride under a Puritan's black bonnet than under Alexander the Great's diadem: a black hat overtopping a crown. Such an image would have had immediate and obvious politico-religious resonances for a contemporary audience. Though Peacham's work augments the emblematic quality of James's prose, it also highlights the aphoristic structure already in place.

The literary precedents to the writing of *Basilikon Doron* are extensive, and serve to indicate the degree to which James's ample scholarly and literary understanding of kingship informed his writings on the subject. Numerous examples of similar texts, or texts that incorporate similar material into their body, exist. Hence, *Basilikon Doron* may be placed within a long tradition of literary antecedents and coevals whose generalized purpose was, as Edmund Spenser states in the letter to Sir Walter Ralegh that prefaces *The Faerie Queene,* "to fashion a gentleman or noble person in virtuous and gentle discipline" (15; modernized). Craigie notes, however, that *Basilikon Doron* is the "last English example of a class of writing [treatises on the training of a prince] once widely practiced all over Western Europe" (*Basilikon Doron* 2.69), and this is yet another of its distinguishing features, both as an historical and a literary document. "[T]hat no earlier work written *in English* had ever aroused such curiosity abroad or had enjoyed so wide a circulation outside the bounds of Great Britain" (*Basilikon Doron* 2.2) also indicates the relative degree of textual significance which may be ascribed to *Basilikon Doron.*

In the preface to his French translation of *Basilikon Doron* (1603) Jean Hotman, Seigneur de Villiers, mentions three Byzantine emperors, Basil I, Constantine VII, and Manuel II, all of whom wrote similar treatises addressed to their respective sons. It is unlikely that James would have known these texts, though, as Craigie notes, their mention by Hotman may have been intended "as a compliment to King James by seeming to put him on a level with these illustrious and royal authors" (*Basilikon Doron* 2.64). Another more likely precedent to James's treatise may have been written by the Holy Roman Emperor Charles V, who also wrote advice to his son, Philip. Charles's advice survived in both state papers and a pseudograph attributed to Charles that James received from Giacomo Castelvetro in manuscript during the latter's stay in Scotland. Whatever its specific provenance, *Basilikon Doron* has a wide range of relations with other well-known texts that address the problems of educating a prince (or courtier) capable of moral self-governance: John of Salisbury's *Policraticus* (*The Statesman's Book,* 1159), Giraldus Cambrensis's *De Principis Instructione Liber* (*The Book of the Instruction of a Prince,* late twelfth century), Thomas Aquinas's *De Regimine Principum* (*On the Rule of Princes,* c. 1265), Petrarch's *De Republica Optime Administranda* (*Concerning the Best Administered Republic,* mid-fourteenth century), the seventh book of John Gower's *Confessio Amantis* (*The Lover's Confession,* c. 1386), Stephen Baron's *De Regimine Principum* (1509), Joachim Du Bellay's *Discours au Roi* (*Speech to the King,* 1556), Pierre Ronsard's *L'Institution pour l'adolescence du Roy* (*The Rules of Government for the Adolescence of the King,* 1562), Baldassare Castiglione's *Il Cortegiano* (*The Book of the Courtier,* translated into English by Sir Thomas Hoby in 1561), Niccolò Machiavelli's *Il Principe* (*The Prince,* 1513; not translated into English until 1640), Sir Thomas Elyot's *The Book Named the Governor* (1531), Roger Ascham's *The Scholemaster* (1570), Edmund Spenser's *The Faerie Queene* (1596), and James Cleland's *The Introduction of a Young Nobleman* (1611; originally published in 1607 under a different title).

Though such a listing is far from exhaustive, it demonstrates the historical and cultural amplitude of the literary contexts encompassed by James in his writing of *Basilikon Doron.* The skilled manipulation of an extensive historical and literary tradition was (and still is) impressive, and no doubt served James well in validating both his authority as Scottish sovereign and his claim to the English throne. Direct evidence of intertextual practices in *Basilikon Doron* may be found in the sidebar notes included in the 1603 and 1616 editions and in connections that readers will draw between James's and others' texts. In *The Prince,* for example, Machiavelli counsels that "[a] prince ought also to show himself an admirer of talent [*virtù*], giving recognition to men of ability [*uomini virtuosi*] and honoring those who excel in a particular art" (65). James puts his own spin on this bit of advice by suggesting in Book Two that Henry "[u]se true liberality in rewarding the good and bestowing frankly for your honour and weal, but with that proportional discretion that every man may be served according to his measure, wherein respect must be had to his rank, deserts, and necessity." What is, in the case of Machiavelli, a rather open-ended notion of showing recognition, becomes, for James, a matter of proportion tempered by "rank, rewards, and necessity." It is tempting to see this as a clever bit of intertextual manipulation, with James outdoing Machiavelli in the craftiness of his advice.

James clearly was not one to adhere blindly to literary or scholarly tradition. In the case of *The Faerie Queene,* for example, though many of its allegorical ideals would have coincided with his own idealized notions of kingship, James took famous exception to a passage in Book V, canto ix, stanzas 25–50. The passage seemed to represent in the most negative allegorical terms his mother, Mary (Duessa), which led to the English ambassador Robert Bowes's report in November of 1596 that "[t]he King has conceived great offense against Edward [sic] Spenser publishing ... some dishonour-able effects ... against himself and his mother deceased. He alleged that this book was passed with privilege of her Majesty's Commis-sioners .... But therein I have (I think) satisfied him that it is not given out with such privilege. Yet he still desires that Edward [sic] Spenser for this fault may be duly tried and punished" (cited in Bergeron 45). Little wonder then that in the third book of *Basilikon Doron,* James took pains to instruct Henry on proper behaviour to his mother in a passage that smacks of a sort of literary retribution against Spenser's insinuations about James and Mary:

> And if it fall out that my wife shall outlive me, as ever you think to purchase my blessing, honour your mother. Set Bathsheba in a throne on your right hand; offend her for nothing, much less wrong her. Remember her, *quæ longa decem tulerit fastidia menses,* and that your flesh and blood is made of hers, and begin not, like the young lords and lairds, your first wars upon your mother, but press earnestly to deserve her blessing. Neither deceive yourself with many that say they care not for their parents' curse so they deserve it not. O invert not the order of nature by judging your superiors, chiefly in your own particular. But assure yourself the blessing or curse of the parents has almost ever a prophetic power joined with it, and if there were no more, honour your parents for the lengthening of your own days, as God in his law promises. Honour also them that are *in loco parentum* unto you, such as your governors,

upbringers, and preceptors. Be thankful unto them and reward them, which is your duty and honour.

The passage resonates strangely because of James's own notable failings and extremely conflicted feelings in "honour[ing]" his own mother (not to mention his wife, Anne of Denmark), and demonstrates the degree to which such intertextual references inform and enrich the understanding of James's texts.

Yet another example of James's independence of mind, particularly with regard to the classical sources that formed the basis of Renaissance humanist practice, is his advice in the third book of *Basilikon Doron* to "write in [Henry's] own language" as a means of exercising his sovereignty over the linguistic imperialism of Latin and Greek, languages of which James opined: "there is nothing left to be said in Greek and Latin already." This somewhat ambiguous comment is typical of James's acute political sensibilities. James's admonition, again in the third book of *Basilikon Doron*, that it "best become a King to purify and make famous his own tongue," though spoken in the Scottish context, is a canny anticipation of the kinds of nationalist and linguistic politics he would have to address in ascending the English throne. Sir Philip Sidney's *A Defence of Poetry* (1595) provides a good example of the national anxieties surrounding the merit of English by comparison with other European languages, anxieties whose potential for political manipulation James no doubt understood: "but for the uttering sweetly and properly the conceits of the mind (which is the end of speech), that hath it [English] equally with any other tongue in the world" (73). It is smart politics to invoke historical tradition to authorize your political ethics while simultaneously seeming to separate yourself from that tradition ("there is nothing left to be said in Greek and Latin already") in order to play to nationalist sentiment about the linguistic viability of either Scots or English.

Basilikon Doron, then, in all its aspects—as princely tutor, compendium of commonplace wisdom, expression of James's personal experience of kingship, and canny political statement—is an enormously rewarding text for students of the early modern period seeking to historicize the literary and intellectual contexts of that period more accurately. Whether or not it represents, as James states in the preface to *Basilikon Doron,* "the true image of my very mind," the work expresses the particular historical and cultural vantage point of a Renaissance sovereign whose political and literary acumen are demonstrably intertwined.

Editorial Note

The True Law of Free Monarchies was first published in Edinburgh in 1598 by the king's printer, Robert Waldegrave. In light of the intense interest in James in 1603, as he was about to ascend the English throne, the book was reprinted in that year in London, using Waldegrave's edition as copy text. In 1616 *The True Law* was included in James's *Workes*, printed in London. These texts are the same in all important points.

Basilikon Doron exists in the British Library in a manuscript in the king's own hand. It was first published by Waldegrave in Edinburgh in 1599 in a private edition of seven copies. In response to criticism from those who were able to obtain this private edition, revisions were made to the text, and this revised edition was published in Scottish and English editions in 1603. The 1603 version of *Basilikon Doron* is the one printed in the 1616 *Workes*. Craigie's edition collates the manuscript and the 1599 and 1603 editions.

The 1603 and 1616 editions omit one of the two original introductory sonnets and add a lengthy preface to the reader, which responds to the earlier criticisms and which is the most important variation to be found in the different editions of *Basilikon Doron*. The 1603 and 1616 editions alter the text throughout, sometimes altering phrasing, more often lengthening the discussion. For instance, in the first book, James adds the discussion of the Book of Kings ("And most properly of any other belongs the reading thereof unto kings ...") and, in the second book, the discussion of "Puritan" opposition to James is significantly altered, the 1599 edition reading,

> And because there was ever some learned and honest men of the ministry that were ashamed of the presumption of these seditious people, there could no way be found out so meet for maintaining their plots, as parity in the Church ... [modernized]

35

The variations among the manuscript and the texts of 1599 and 1603 are mapped exhaustively by Craigie and discussed at some length in the introduction to his edition of *Basilikon Doron* (2.88–116).

We have chosen to use the 1616 folio *Workes* as copy text—what we refer to in our annotations as the "original"—for both *The True Law* and *Basilikon Doron*. In spite of their origins as Scottish texts, our interest is ultimately in James as king of England, and we follow a long tradition, which includes McIlwain, in citing the *Workes* as the standard text of James's English period. The 1616 *Workes* clearly represents an attempt to standardize, in the manner of a collected works, the features of widely divergent writings. It was clearly printed *cum privilegio,* that is with the royal seal of approval, and we can assume, given James's reputation for pedantry, that he had a hand in the choice, order, and shape of the texts that were printed. *The True Law* underwent no significant changes between 1598 and 1616; in the case of *Basilikon Doron,* the *Workes* prints the revised text, which, given its elaborate discussion of James's reception in England, seems to be a more appropriate text for our purposes than the manuscript or the edition of 1599.

The 1616 *Workes* also has the virtue of placing the texts in the new dynastic context which followed on the death of Prince Henry in 1612. James Montagu, Bishop of Winchester, who arranged for the publication, prefaces the book with a letter to the new heir apparent, "The thrice illustrious and most excellent Prince, Charles, the only son of our sovereign lord the King." This letter, echoing Buchanan's dedication of *The Power of the Crown in Scotland* to the young James and James's original dedication of *Basilikon Doron* to Henry, passes the texts to their new heir:

> His Majesty ... wrote his *Basilikon Doron* to Prince Henry, your Highness' most worthy brother; his part, by God his providence, is fallen to your lot, and who may justly detain you from the rest?

The new *Workes* are placed before Charles as precept just as *Basilikon Doron* had itself been placed before Henry: "Let these *Workes* therefore, most gracious prince, lie before you as a pattern; you cannot have a better." What Charles did with his inheritance is, of course, another chapter in English history.

Beginning in 1603, *Basilikon Doron* was printed with extensive side-notes: subject headings, references, and occasional topical allusions. It is not clear who provided these notes, whether James, an editor, or both. Since the subject headings provide no information not found in the text itself, we have, for the sake of readability, omitted them. Biblical references, which appear in the 1599 edition, and in all editions of *The True Law,* have been transferred to footnotes and, where these references are mistaken, silently corrected. Other references, mainly to classical sources such as Plato, Aristotle, Cicero, Quintilian, Isocrates, and Xenophon, have been omitted, except in a few pressing instances where they appear in footnotes. To have included all these references, many of which are vague and untraceable, would have encumbered the reading of the text to a degree we think unwarranted. We regret that this omission obscures the text's elaborate and learned distillation of classical advice on kingship and governance and urge the reader to consult Craigie's apparatus for more elaborate references. Direct quotations have been noted and references have been clarified and occasionally corrected. When side-notes raise interesting topical allusions, these have been referred to in footnotes.

We have modernized the text throughout. In the process of doing so, we have come to realize how labyrinthine are the second-guessing and compromise this involves. Editors who provide a modernized version of a Renaissance text of necessity impose new structures—syntactic, metrical, semantic—all of which contribute to the edited text being a reading, of sorts, of the base text. In this last regard, the glosses and annotations we have provided should be read as helpful but not necessarily definitive indications of James's meaning and context. After much thought and debate we have decided upon the following procedures, hoping thereby to make the texts more accessible and readable for contemporary students of politics, history, and literature.

Spelling has been modernized throughout, except in the case of archaisms without corresponding modern forms; in these cases we have adopted standardized spelling from the Oxford English Dictionary (OED). Biblical, classical, and historical names have also been modernized. We have used King James's Authorized Version of the Bible (1611) in our notes on relevant biblical passages. Readers should bear in mind, however, that James himself made use of a different version of the Bible in his writing of these two texts, most likely the Bassandyne Bible (1579), which was based on the Geneva Bible (1560). We have retained archaic pronoun and verb forms, a decision that led to much debate, but one which we feel will allow readers to experience much of the distinctive flavour of late sixteenth-century prose. The use of italics and capitalization has been modernized; we have retained capitalization for words referring to groups of people ("Puritan," "Anabaptist") and for "God" and "Scripture." Quotations from Greek have been transliterated. The historical designations BCE and CE, as opposed to BC and AD, have been used, another decision that sparked debate. We see our edition as a secular, late twentieth-century edition rather than one following the spirit of James's time and outlook—this is apparent from the critical tone of many of our notes. We hope we have been sensitive enough not to ride roughshod over James's beliefs, but have decided, ultimately, that religiously neutral designations, especially as they appear only tangentially and in notes, have the most integrity for us.

On occasion James's syntax simply does not work in a way that modern rules of punctuation can cope with, but as far as possible, punctuation, including procedures for quotation, has been modernized. Where modern punctuation collides with sixteenth-century practice in a manner that may leave the reader puzzled, we have chosen to annotate in a way that will give the reader some possibilities for coming to a decision about James's meaning. Although this modernization sometimes (and regrettably) distorts the cadences of James's prose, it has the benefit of making the syntax and logic of the sentences much more accessible. In a few instances of obviously faulty grammar or notable omission of words, we have inserted our reading in square brackets in the body of the text. For the purpose of consistency, we have modernized, using the same principles, all citations from early modern texts that appear in notes. Where this is not the case, as in all Shakespeare citations, we have used a standard scholarly edition or, when a citation has not been modernized in the body of a critical commentary we cite, the integrity of the passage has been maintained. To avoid any confusion in this regard all passages in the notes where modernization has occurred are clearly indicated. The selected bibliography contains a listing of key texts we have used in preparing this edition; where other sources have been used to provide information in an annotation, full bibliographical information is given in the note itself. Finally, for the sake of convenience we have provided, at their first appearance in each text, footnote definitions of words that may give the modern reader trouble, and have provided a glossary of these words as well for ease of reference.

Modernizing James's text in the way we have does, admittedly, change it. Those who are concerned about these changes should consult the 1616 *Workes* or the editions of McIlwain or Craigie. For the sake of a brief comparison with our own text, here is the "Advertisement to the Reader," from *The True Law,* as it appears in the original:

> Accept, J pray you (my deare countreymen) as thankefully this Pamphlet that J offer vnto you, as louingly it is written for your weale. J would be loath both to be faſchious, and fectleſſe: And therefore, if it be not ſententious, at least it is ſhort. Jt may be yee miſſe many things that yee looke for in it: But for excuſe thereof, conſsider rightly that I onely lay downe herein the trew grounds, to teach you the right-way, without wasting time vpon refuting the aduerſsaries. And yet I trust, if ye will take narrow tent, ye ſhall finde moſt of their great gunnes payed home againe, either with contrary concluſions, or tacite obiections, ſuppoſe in a dairned forme, and indirectly: For my intention is to instruct, and not irritat, if J may eſchew it. The profite I would wiſh you to make of it, is, as well ſo to frame all your actions according to theſe grounds, as may confirme you in the courſe of honest and obedient Subiects to your King in all times comming, as alſo, when ye ſhall fall in purpoſe with any that ſhall praiſe or excuſe the by-past rebellions that brake foorth either in this countrey, or in any other, ye ſhall herewith bee armed against their Sirene ſongs, laying their particular examples to the ſquare of theſe grounds. Whereby yee ſhall ſoundly keepe the courſe of righteous Judgement, decerning wiſely of euery action onely according to the qualitie thereof, and not according to your preiudged conceits of the committers: So ſhall ye, by reaping profit to your ſelves, turne my paine into pleaſure. But least the whole Pamphlet runne out at the gaping mouth of this Preface, if it were any more enlarged; I end, with committing you to God, and me to your charitable cenſures. (*Workes* 191–92; in italics)

Finally, as editors we can lay claim neither to objectivity nor to ahistoricity, but recognize that the production of these texts in modernized versions has a great deal to do with our own positions as subjects with particular histories, not to mention particular "senses" of history. In this regard, we align ourselves with Michel Foucault's assertion that "[t]he more History attempts to transcend its own rootedness in historicity, and the greater the efforts it makes to attain, beyond the historical relativity of its origins and its choices, the sphere of universality, the more clearly it bears the marks of its historical birth, and the more evidently there appears through it the history of which it is itself a part ..." (*The Order of Things* 371). We would expect our readers to be operating out of similar recognitions, however dissimilar their subjectivities or histories. In short, the truism that no editorial decision, no interpretive decision, is neutral holds for our readings of James as much as it does for other readers of James, as much as it does for James's original editorial decisions. The virtue of careful editing was something to which James himself was keenly attuned, as he mentions in the third book of *Basilikon Doron*:

> Flatter not yourself in your labours, but before they be set forth, let them first be privily censured by some of the best skilled men in that craft that in these works ye meddle with. And because your writs will remain as true pictures of your mind to all posterities, let them be free of all uncomeliness and unhonesty .... I mean both your verse and your prose, letting first that fury and heat wherewith they were written cool at leisure, and then, as an uncouth judge and censor, revising them over again before they be published .... (*Workes* 184–85)

The "true pictures of your mind" associated with the act of writing, or rather with the acts of representation to which writing is only a clue, is a figure of speech that assumes that such "true pictures" exist. As editors we have felt it to be a small part of our job to expose, in two of James's crucial political acts of textual representation, the rather large gap between the "truth" proferred as self-evident by James, and the "truth" that emerges from a close reading of the ambiguities and discontinuities in James's texts. Perhaps somewhere between the two "truths" lies another version of the truth.

Selected Bibliography

Akrigg, G. P. V., ed. *Letters of King James VI & I.* Berkeley: U of California P, 1984.

Allen, J. W. *A History of Political Thought in the Sixteenth Century.* London: Methuen, 1957. [1928].

Altman, Joel T. *The Tudor Play of Mind: Rhetorical Inquiry and the Development of Elizabethan Drama.* Berkeley: U of California P, 1978.

Ashton, Robert, ed. *James I by His Contemporaries.* London: Hutchinson, 1969.

Barroll, Leeds. *Politics, Plague, and Shakespeare's Theater: The Stuart Years.* Ithaca: Cornell UP, 1991.

Bergeron, David M. *Royal Family, Royal Lovers: King James of England and Scotland.* Columbia: U of Missouri P, 1991.

Bingham, Caroline. *The Making of a King: The Early Years of James VI and I.* London: Collins, 1968.

Birch, Thomas, ed. *The Court and Times of James the First.* London: Henry Colburn, 1849.

Brown, Jennifer M. (Jenny Wormald). "Scottish Politics 1567–1625." *The Reign of James VI and I.* Ed. Alan G. R. Smith. London: Macmillan, 1973.

Bruce, John, ed. *Correspondence of King James VI. of Scotland with Sir Robert Cecil and Others in England.* London: The Camden Society, 1861.

———, ed. *Letters of Queen Elizabeth and King James VI. of Scotland.* London: The Camden Society, 1849.

Buchanan, George. *The Powers of the Crown in Scotland.* Tr. Charles Flinn Arrowood. Austin: U of Texas P, 1949.

Burgess, Glenn. "The Divine Right of Kings Reconsidered." *English Historical Review* 425 (October 1992): 837–61.

————. *The Politics of the Ancient Constitution: An Introduction to English Political Thought, 1603–1642.* University Park, Pa.: Pennsylvania State UP, 1993.

Christianson, Paul. "Royal and Parliamentary Voices on the Ancient Constitution, c. 1604–1621." *The Mental World of the Jacobean Court.* Ed. Linda Levy Peck. Cambridge: Cambridge UP, 1991: 71–95.

Collier, Susanne. "Recent Studies in James VI and I." *English Literary Renaissance* 23.3 (1993): 509–19.

Coprario, John. "Songs of Mourning (1613)." *The English Lute-Songs.* 1.17. Eds. Gerald Hendrie and Thurston Dart. London: Stainer & Bell, 1959.

Craigie, James, ed. *The Basilicon Doron of King James VI.* 2 vols. Edinburgh: William Blackwood & Sons, 1944, 1950.

————, ed. *Minor Prose Works of King James VI and I.* Edinburgh: Scottish Text Society, 1982.

————, ed. *The Poems of James VI. of Scotland.* 2 vols. Edinburgh: William Blackwood & Sons, 1955, 1958.

Daly, James. "The Idea of Absolute Monarchy in Seventeenth Century England." *Historical Journal* 21 (1978): 227–50.

Doelman, James. "'A King of Thine Own Heart': The English Reception of King James VI and I's *Basilikon Doron.*" *Seventeenth Century* 9.1 (Spring 1994): 1–9.

Fischlin, Daniel. "The 'Candie-souldier,' Venice, and James VI (I)'s Advice on Monarchic Dress in *Basilikon Doron.*" *Notes & Queries* 240 of the continuous series [New Series, 42].3 (September 1995): 357–61.

————. "'Counterfeiting God': James VI (I) and the Politics of *Dæmonologie.*" *Journal of Narrative Technique* 26.1 (1996): 1–29.

Figgis, John Neville. *The Divine Right of Kings.* New York: Harper & Row, 1965. [1914].

Foucault, Michel. *The Order of Things: An Archaeology of the Human Sciences.* New York: Vintage Books, 1970.

Fraser, Antonia. *King James.* New York: Alfred Knopf, 1975.

Galloway, Bruce. *The Union of England and Scotland 1603–1608.* Edinburgh: John Donald Publishers, 1986.

Goldberg, Jonathan. *James I and the Politics of Literature.* Stanford: Stanford UP, 1989.

Harrison, G. B., ed. *The Letters of Queen Elizabeth I*. New York: Funk & Wagnalls, 1968.

Harrison, Wilfrid. *Conflict and Compromise: History of British Political Thought 1593–1900*. New York: Free Press, 1965.

Henshall, Nicholas. *The Myth of Absolutism: Change and Continuity in Early Modern European Monarchy*. London: Longman, 1992.

Houston, S. J. *James I*. London: Longman, 1973.

James I. *The Workes* (1616) [STC 14344]. Rpt. Hildesheim: Georg Olms Verlag, 1971.

Kantorowicz, Ernst H. *The King's Two Bodies: A Study in Medieval Political Theology*. Princeton: Princeton UP, 1957.

Kimmel, Michael S. *Absolutism and Its Discontents: State and Society in Seventeenth-Century France and England*. New Brunswick, NJ: Transaction Books, 1988.

King, Preston. *The Ideology of Order: A Comparative Analysis of Jean Bodin and Thomas Hobbes*. London: George Allen & Unwin, 1974.

Lee, Maurice Jr. *Government by Pen: Scotland under James VI and I*. Urbana: U of Illinois P, 1980.

———. *Great Britain's Solomon: James VI and I in His Three Kingdoms*. Urbana: U of Illinois P, 1990.

Machiavelli, Niccolò. *The Prince*. Tr. Robert M. Adams. New York: Norton, 1977.

Maidment, J., ed. *Letters and State Papers During the Reign of King James the Sixth chiefly from the Manuscript Collections of Sir James Balfour of Denmyln*. Edinburgh: Edinburgh Printing Company, 1838.

Mathew, David. *James I*. London: Eyre and Spottiswoode, 1967.

McElwee, William. *The Wisest Fool in Christendom: The Reign of King James I and VI*. London: Faber and Faber, 1958.

McIlwain, Charles H., ed. *The Political Works of James I*. New York: Russell and Russell, 1965.

Nichols, John. *The Progresses, Processions, and Magnificent Festivities of King James the First, His Royal Consort, Family, and Court*. London: Society of Antiquaries, 1828.

Norbrook, David. "*Macbeth* and the Politics of Historiography." *Politics of Discourse: The Literature and History of Seventeenth-Century England*. Eds. Kevin Sharpe and Steven N. Zwicker. Berkeley: U of California P, 1987: 78–116.

Passingham, W. J. *A History of the Coronation.* London: Sampson Low, Marston & Co., n.d.

Peck, Linda Levy, ed. *The Mental World of the Jacobean Court.* Cambridge: Cambridge UP, 1991.

Robertson, William. *The History of Scotland during the reigns of Queen Mary and of King James VI till his accession to the Crown of England.* 2 vols. London, 1761.

Russell, Conrad. *The Causes of the English Civil War.* Oxford: Clarendon Press, 1990.

———. "Divine Rights in the Early Seventeenth Century." *Public Duty and Private Conscience in Seventeenth-Century England: Essays Presented to G. E. Aylmer.* Eds. John Morrill, Paul Slack, and Daniel Woolf. Oxford: Clarendon Press, 1993: 101–20.

———. *The Fall of the British Monarchies, 1637–1642.* Oxford: Clarendon Press, 1991.

———. *Parliaments and English Politics, 1621–1629.* Oxford: Clarendon Press, 1979.

Rypins, Stanley. "The Printing of *Basilikòn Dôron,* 1603." *Papers of the Bibliographical Society of America* 64 (1970): 393–417.

Sabine, George H. *A History of Political Theory.* Rev. Thomas Landon Thorson. 4th Edition. Fort Worth: Holt, Rinehart and Winston, 1973.

Salmon, J. H. M. "James I, the Oath of Allegiance, the Venetian Interdict, and the Reappearance of French Ultramontanism." *The Cambridge History of Political Thought, 1450–1700.* Eds. J. H. Burns and Mark Goldie. Cambridge: Cambridge UP, 1991: 247–53.

Scott, Otto J. *James I.* New York: Mason/Charter, 1976.

Shakespeare, William. *The Riverside Shakespeare.* Ed. G. Blakemore Evans. Boston: Houghton Mifflin, 1974.

Sharpe, Kevin. *Politics and Ideas in Early Stuart England.* London: Pinter, 1989.

———. "Private Conscience and Public Duty in the Writings of James VI and I." *Public Duty and Private Conscience in Seventeenth-Century England: Essays Presented to G. E. Aylmer.* Eds. John Morrill, Paul Slack, and Daniel Woolf. Oxford: Clarendon Press, 1993: 77–100.

Sidney, Sir Philip. *A Defence of Poetry.* Ed. J. A. Van Dorsten. Oxford: Oxford UP, 1988.

Smith, Alan G. R., ed. *The Reign of James VI and I*. London: Macmillan, 1973.

Sommerville, J. P. "Absolutism and Royalism." *The Cambridge History of Political Thought, 1450–1700*. Eds. J. H. Burns and Mark Goldie. Cambridge: Cambridge UP, 1991: 347–73.

———. *Politics and Ideology in England, 1603–1640*. London: Longman, 1986.

———. "James I and the Divine Right of Kings: English Politics and Continental Theory." *The Mental World of the Jacobean Court*. Ed. Linda Levy Peck. Cambridge: Cambridge UP, 1991: 55–70.

———, ed. *James VI and I: Political Writings*. Cambridge: Cambridge UP, 1994.

Spenser, Edmund. *The Faerie Queene*. Ed. Thomas P. Roche, Jr. with C. Patrick O'Donnell, Jr. New Haven: Yale UP, 1981.

Strong, Roy. *Henry, Prince of Wales and England's Lost Renaissance*. London: Thames and Hudson, 1986.

Walter, David. *James I*. Sussex: Wayland Publishers, 1975.

Willson, David Harris. *King James VI and I*. London: Jonathan Cape, 1959.

Wootton, David, ed. *Divine Right and Democracy: An Anthology of Political Writing in Stuart England*. Harmondsworth: Penguin, 1986.

Wormald, Jenny. "James VI and I, *Basilikon Doron* and *The Trew Law of Free Monarchies:* The Scottish Context and the English Translation." *The Mental World of the Jacobean Court*. Ed. Linda Levy Peck. Cambridge: Cambridge UP, 1991: 36–54.

———. *Court, Kirk and Community: Scotland 1470–1625*. New York: Columbia UP, 1991.

The True Law of Free Monarchies: or
The Reciprock and Mutual Duty
Betwixt a Free King
and his Natural Subjects

An Advertisement
To the Reader

Accept, I pray you, my dear countrymen, as thankfully this pamphlet that I offer unto you as lovingly it is written for your weal.[1] I would be loath both to be fashious[2] and feckless.[3] And therefore, if it be not sententious, at least it is short. It may be ye miss many things that ye look for in it. But for excuse thereof, consider rightly that I only lay down herein the true grounds to teach you the right way, without wasting time upon refuting the adversaries. And yet I trust if ye will take narrow tent,[4] ye shall find most of their great guns paid home[5] again, either with contrary conclusions or tacit objections, suppose in a dairned[6] form and indirectly. For my intention is to instruct and not irritate, if I may eschew it. The profit I would wish you to make of it is as well so to frame all your actions according to these grounds as may confirm you in the course of honest and obedient subjects to your king in all times coming as also, when ye shall fall in purpose with any that shall praise or excuse the by-past rebellions that [broke][7] forth either in this country or in any other, ye shall herewith be armed against their siren songs, laying their particular examples to the square[8] of these grounds. Whereby ye shall soundly keep the course of righteous judgement, decerning[9] wisely of every action only according to the quality thereof and not according to your prejudged conceits of the committers. So shall ye, by reaping profit to yourselves, turn my pain into pleasure. But lest the whole pam-

---

[1] welfare

[2] vexatious

[3] futile, ineffectual

[4] to give close heed to

[5] avenged, repaid in full

[6] secret, hidden

[7] "brake" in original

[8] the instrument by which a carpenter measures the accuracy of his or her work, used here in the sense of guiding principle or measure

[9] pronouncing judgement

phlet run out at the gaping mouth of this preface, if it were any more enlarged, I end with committing you to God and me to your charitable censures.

C. *Philopatris*[10]

---

[10]"One who loves his country"; in Greek letters in original. The "C." may represent, as Craigie points out, the Latin word "Caledonius," that is, a Caledonian or a Scot.

The True Law of Free Monarchies: or The Reciprock[11] and Mutual Duty Betwixt a Free King and His Natural Subjects

As there is not a thing so necessary to be known by the people of any land, next the knowledge of their God, as the right knowledge of their allegiance according to the form of government established among them, especially in a monarchy (which form of government, as resembling the divinity, approacheth nearest to perfection, as all the learned and wise men from the beginning have agreed upon, unity being the perfection of all things), so hath the ignorance and (which is worse) the seduced opinion of the multitude, blinded by them who think themselves able to teach and instruct the ignorants, procured the wrack[12] and overthrow of sundry flourishing commonwealths and heaped heavy calamities threatening utter destruction upon others. And the smiling success that unlawful rebellions have oftentimes had against princes in ages past (such hath been the misery and iniquity of the time) hath by way of practice strengthened many in their error, albeit there cannot be a more deceivable argument than to judge aye[13] the justness of the cause by the event thereof, as hereafter shall be proved more at length. And among others, no commonwealth that ever hath been since the beginning hath had greater need of the true knowledge of this ground than this our so long disordered and distracted commonwealth hath, the misknowledge hereof being the only spring from whence have flowed so many endless calamities, miseries, and confusions, as is better felt by many than the cause thereof well known and deeply considered. The natural zeal, therefore, that I bear to this my native country, with the great pity I have to see the so long disturbance thereof for lack of the true knowledge of this ground (as I have said before), hath compelled me at last to break silence, to discharge my conscience to you my dear countrymen herein, that, knowing the ground from whence these your many endless troubles have proceeded, as well as ye have already too long tasted the bitter fruits thereof, ye may by knowledge

---

[11] reciprocal
[12] ruin
[13] ever

and eschewing of the cause escape and divert the lamentable effects that ever necessarily follow thereupon. I have chosen, then, only to set down in this short treatise the true grounds of the mutual duty and allegiance betwixt a free and absolute monarch and his people, not to trouble your patience with answering the contrary propositions which some[14] have not been ashamed to set down in writ,[15] to the poisoning of infinite number of simple souls and their own perpetual and well deserved infamy. For by answering them, I could not have eschewed whiles[16] to pick and bite well saltly[17] their persons, which would rather have bred contentiousness among the readers (as they had liked or misliked) than found instruction of the truth, which, I protest to him that is the searcher of all hearts,[18] is the only mark that I shoot at herein.

First, then, I will set down the true grounds whereupon I am to build out of the Scriptures, since monarchy is the true pattern of divinity, as I have already said; next, from the fundamental laws of our own kingdom, which nearest must concern us; thirdly, from the law of nature by divers[19] similitudes drawn out of the same; and will conclude syne[20] by answering the most weighty and appearing incommodities[21] that can be objected.

---

[14]James is referring to contemporary writings that attack the notions of kingship, succession, divine right, and absolutism. For a recent explanation of the kinds of opposition James was facing, see Maurice Lee Jr.'s *Great Britain's Solomon*, especially chapter three, "Kingship and Kingcraft," 63–92. At the time of the writing of *The True Law*, James was subject to enormous political pressure regarding his right to succession to the throne of England and his relations with the kirk. In May of 1592 there had been a confrontation between James and a delegation of ministers in which the "king complained that the ministers were preaching favorably about Knox, Buchanan, and the Regent Moray, 'who,' said he, 'could not be defended but by traitorous and seditious theologues [theologians]'" (*Great Britain's Solomon* 74). Lee argues that "James's preoccupations in 1598 determined both what he had to say in *The Trew Law* and *Basilicon Doron* and how he said it ... the main thrust of *The Trew Law* was directed against the pretensions of Andrew Melville [a well-known opponent of James who denounced the episcopal polity and was highly sceptical of the secular authority of kings] and his ilk on the one hand and, on the other, against objections to the doctrine of indefeasible hereditary right, whether those of George Buchanan, the Jesuit Robert Persons, whose attack on the right of a heretic to succeed to the English throne appeared in 1594, or the contract theorists, who placed so much emphasis on the coronation oath" (82–3). The passage may be making an oblique catch-all reference to all of these makers of "contrary propositions" who presented threats to the stability and sustainability of James's reign.

[15]writing

[16]on occasion

[17]to make pay very dearly, that is, to attack

[18]oblique reference to God

[19]sundry, several

[20]thereafter

[21]the most apparent and hurtful or injurious things

The prince's duty to his subjects is so clearly set down in many places of the Scriptures and so openly confessed by all the good princes according to their oath in their coronation[22] as, not needing to be long therein, I shall as shortly as I can run through it.

------

[22] See Craigie's *Minor Prose,* 129–32, for further information on the Scottish coronation oath that the Earl of Morton took for James when James was only thirteen months old, on July 19, 1567. Both the Scottish and the English oaths begin with a recognition of the king's relation to God, the Scottish oath making mention of the king's duty to "maintain the true religion of Jesus Christ" and to abolish all "false religion contrary to the same" (*Minor Prose* 131; modernized). The protocols of the English coronation oath are described in detail in the *Liber Regalis,* which dates from 1307, just prior to the coronation of Edward II. James I, despite the many changes in the protocol of the event, apparently "insisted on the entire original ceremony and ritual of the *Liber Regalis* for his Coronation" (W. J. Passingham, *A History of the Coronation* [London: Sampson Low, Marston & Co., n.d.], 106). Modern coronations follow the basic structures set out in the *Liber Regalis.* The oath itself, as set out in the "original manuscript of Abbot Litlington" (106) follows more or less the following form:

> The Archbishop of Canterbury shall demand of the king, saying, "Pleaseth it you to confirm and observe the laws of ancient times, granted from God by just and devout kings unto the English nation, by Oath, unto the said people, especially the laws, customs, and liberties granted unto the church and laity by the famous King Edward (the Confessor)?"
>
> The king answering that he will perform and observe all the promises, then shall the Archbishop read unto him the articles, whereunto he shall swear thus, saying:—
>
> "Thou shalt procure unto the church of God, unto the clergy, and people, firm peace and unity in God, according to thy power."
>
> He shall answer, "I will perform it."
>
> "Art thou pleased to be administered in all thy judgments indifferent and upright justice, and to use discretion with mercy and verity?"
>
> He shall answer, "I grant and promise." (109–10)

Oddly enough, Passingham states that "the exact words of the Oath are nowhere set out in the original manuscript of the *Liber Regalis*" (120). James included, as the last text in the 1616 *Workes, A Paterne for a Kings Inauguration* in which he sums up the political and contractual "signification" of an inauguration:

> A king hath first great cause of contentment if the people of all sorts, especially those to whose place it belongs, do willingly convene and concur to his public inauguration. A king must look to have that action performed in public and in a public place that the love of his people may appear in that solemn action. Two things a king hath specially to look unto at his inauguration: first, that his title to the crown be just, and next that he may possess it with the love of his people. For although a monarchy or hereditary kingdom cannot justly be denied to the lawful successor, whatever the affections of the people be, yet it is a great sign of the blessing of God when he enters in it with the willing applause of his subjects. (*Workes* 621–22; modernized)

Kings[23] are called gods by the prophetical King David[24] because they sit upon God his throne in the earth and have the count of their

---

[23]The following paragraph uses a number of paraphrases from Scripture, though, as printed in the 1616 folio, these paraphrases seem to be direct citation. Several possibilities exist for explaining the nature of the obscurities in this passage. First, James may have been citing from a faulty memory; secondly, the printer may have mistaken paraphrase for direct citation; thirdly, and perhaps most likely given the nature of James's tendentious arguments, James may have reproduced the passages according to the hermeneutics of absolutism, that is, according to an exegetical method that suited his purpose of arguing toward the divine right of kings. The way in which paraphrase suits James's argument is exemplified in his paraphrase of 1 Samuel 8:19–20, which compares the king to "a good pastor ... [who goes] out and in before his people." In fact, the passage reads "Nevertheless the people refused to obey the voice of Samuel; and they said, Nay; but we will have a king over us; That we also may be like all the nations; and that our king may judge us, and go out before us, and fight our battles." James revises this passage in two ways, the first converting a negative trope of disobedience (to Samuel's prophecy which warns of the oppressions that will be foisted on the people by a king) to a trope of submission to a pastor, and the second diminishing the actual role played by the king in fighting battles for the people, something about which James counsels his son Henry in the second book of *Basilikon Doron*: "And once or twice in your own person hazard yourself fairly [in battle]; but having acquired so the fame of courage and magnanimity, make not a daily soldier of yourself, exposing rashly your person to every peril; but conserve yourself thereafter for the weal of your people, for whose sake ye must more care for yourself than for your own." James's use of the trope of the pastor in his paraphrase is worth noting as is his mention of David in the same paragraph, as if an easy conflation of David and Samuel is possible. In fact, the biblical texts stress David's leadership role and his absolutism as opposed to his "shepherd" or pastoral qualities. The tortuous rhetoric and logic of James's counsel to Henry clearly stages the need for self-preservation at all costs under the guise of an altruistic concern for the people's weal.

[24]Psalm 82:6; Craigie accurately indicates that "[t]he 'because' clause which follows is James's explanation of why this should be so, and is not to be found either in the passage referred to or at any other place in Scripture" (*Minor Prose* 128). Scriptural revisionism is a crucial aspect of James's strategy of accruing authority in the textual representation of absolute power. Like essentializing notions of the "true law," Scripture presented an essential and "true" source of the connections between the divine and the monarch, despite the fact that Scripture often indicates considerable anxiety and scepticism about monarchic rule. See John Bright, *A History of Israel* (Philadelphia: Westminster Press, n.d.), especially Part Three, "Israel Under the Monarchy," and Part Four, "The Monarchy (Continued)." Bright argues that "[t]he monarchy [in Israel] ... never escaped tension. Neither David nor Solomon had, for all their brilliance, succeeded in solving its fundamental problem—essentially that of bridging the gap between tribal independence and the demands of central authority" (207). For further and more recent commentary see P. Kyle McCarter, Jr.'s analysis of 1 Samuel 8:1–22, especially its relationship to Deuteronomy 17:14–17, in the *Anchor Bible 1 Samuel* (Garden City, N. Y.: Doubleday, 1980), 159–62. McCarter says that both the passage from Samuel and Deuteronomy

administration to give unto him. Their office is "to minister justice and judgement to the people,"[25] as the same David saith; "to advance the good and punish the evil,"[26] as he likewise saith; "to establish good laws to his people and procure obedience to the same,"[27] as divers good kings of Judah did; "to procure the peace of the people,"[28] as the same David saith; "to decide all the controversies that can arise among them,"[29] as Solomon[30] did; "to be the minister of God for the weal of them that do well and, as the minister of God, to take vengeance upon them that do evil,"[31] as Saint Paul[32] saith; and finally, "as a good pastor, to go out and in before his people,"[33] as is said in

---

"view monarchy as an institution that tends to become corrupt and must be introduced with much circumspection" (162). McCarter also states that Samuel represents a "sardonic commentary on kingship couched in phrases that combine the genres of curse, oracle, and paternal instruction" (162). See also Joel Rosenberg's "1 and 2 Samuel," *The Literary Guide to the Bible,* eds. Robert Alter and Frank Kermode (Cambridge: Harvard UP, 1987), 122–45, especially his comment that in Samuel "the tradition's ambivalence about kingship is allowed free expression" (127). The problems of Israel, as a religio-political entity, in balancing central authority with the competing demands of various families, tribes, and religious institutions were familiar to James as king of Scotland, who had to deal with what Maurice Lee Jr. calls "aristocratic feuds" (*Government by Pen* 10) from the beginning of his reign, not to mention the ever-present religious issues that colour so much of late sixteenth-century politics.

[25] Psalm 101

[26] Psalm 101

[27] 2 Kings 18:3, 22:2, 23:3; 2 Chronicles 29:2, 34:2, 35:26–27

[28] Psalm 72:7

[29] 1 Kings 3:9

[30] Solomon was the son of David and king of Israel. James, as is common practice, cites Solomon as an example of wisdom, the gift that Solomon was granted by God along with longevity and wealth. See 1 Kings 1–11; 1 Chronicles 22, 23, 28, 29 and 2 Chronicles 1–9. Note that throughout the annotations to both *The True Law* and *Basilikon Doron,* dates given for biblical figures are, in certain cases, approximations based on recent scholarship.

[31] Romans 13:4

[32] Saint Paul (CE c. 5–64) is known for his journeys as an early Christian missionary (through Cyprus, Asia Minor, and the Mediterranean world), for his letters (particularly "The Epistle of Paul the Apostle to the Romans"), and for the tenacity of his faith and his belief in justification through faith, grace, and works (see Acts 8–28).

[33] 1 Samuel 8:19–20

the first of Samuel,[34] "that through the prince's prosperity the people's peace may be procured," as Jeremiah saith.[35]

And therefore, in the coronation of our own kings as well as of every Christian monarch, they give their oath first to maintain the religion presently professed within their country, according to their laws whereby it is established, and to punish all those that should press to alter or disturb the profession thereof; and next to maintain all the lowable[36] and good laws made by their predecessors, to see them put in execution and the breakers and violators thereof to be punished according to the tenor of the same; and lastly to maintain the whole country and every state therein in all their ancient privileges and liberties, as well against all foreign enemies as among themselves; and shortly, to procure the weal and flourishing of his people, not only in maintaining and putting to execution the old lowable laws of the country and by establishing of new as necessity and evil manners will require, but by all other means possible to foresee and prevent all dangers that are likely to fall upon them, and to maintain concord, wealth, and civility among them, as a loving father and careful watchman, caring for them more than for himself, knowing himself to be ordained for them and they not for him, and therefore countable[37] to that great God who placed him as his

---

[34]Samuel was a composite figure, a prophet, priest, and judge of Israel, appointed by God to redeem the Israelites from the consequences of their sins. He was responsible for inaugurating Israel's first two kings, Saul and David. Under Samuel's leadership Israel had several military successes against the Philistines after they had captured the Ark of the Covenant. Samuel is central to James's political and religious symbology in *The True Law*, a fact made all the more interesting by Samuel's resistance to and scepticism about the notion of monarchic authority. See 1 Samuel 1–4, 7–13, 15, 16, 25, 28.

[35]Jeremiah 29:7; Jeremiah was a prophet who lived most of his life in Jerusalem during the decline of the kingdom of Judah in the seventh century BCE (c. 626–586 BCE). He foretold and welcomed the destruction of Jerusalem by Babylon. See Jeremiah; Lamentations; Baruch; and 2 Chronicles 36. Note James's extensive use of paraphrase as opposed to direct citation throughout this paragraph.

[36]permissible, desirable, commendable; the OED cites Charles I's *Large Declaration Concerning the Tumults in Scotland* (1639) as an example of this usage: "According to the lowable lawes and constitutions received in this Realm." William T. Dobson, in the *History of the Bassandyne Bible* (Edinburgh: William Blackwood and Sons, 1887) states: "The tumults referred to in Charles I's 'Large Declaration' were the results of the attempts begun by James VI. to introduce the Episcopal service into Scotland, because it was thought dangerous to the English Church that a form of worship resembling that of the Puritans should exist in any part of the King's dominions" (172).

[37]accountable

lieutenant over them upon the peril of his soul to procure the weal of both souls and bodies, as far as in him lieth, of all them that are committed to his charge. And this oath in the coronation is the clearest civil and fundamental law whereby the king's office is properly defined.

By the law of nature, the king becomes a natural father to all his lieges at his coronation. And as the father of his fatherly duty is bound to care for the nourishing, education, and virtuous government of his children, even so is the king bound to care for all his subjects. As all the toil and pain that the father can take for his children will be thought light and well bestowed by him so that the effect thereof redound to their profit and weal, so ought the prince to do towards his people. As the kindly father ought to foresee all inconvenients[38] and dangers that may arise towards his children and though with the hazard of his own person press to prevent the same, so ought the king towards his people. As the father's wrath and correction upon any of his children that offendeth ought to be by a fatherly chastisement seasoned with pity as long as there is any hope of amendment in them, so ought the king towards any of his lieges that offend in that measure. And shortly, as the father's chief joy ought to be in procuring his children's welfare, rejoicing at their weal, sorrowing and pitying at their evil, to hazard for their safety, travail[39] for their rest, wake for their sleep, and in a word, to think that his earthly felicity and life standeth and liveth more in them nor in himself, so ought a good prince think of his people.

As to the other branch of this mutual and reciprock band[40] is the duty and allegiance that the lieges owe to their king, the ground whereof I take out of the words of Samuel, dited[41] by God's spirit, when God had given him commandment to hear the people's voice in choosing and anointing them a king.[42] And because that place of

---

[38] inconveniences

[39] labour; "travell" in original

[40] that which restrains, binds together, connects, or unites

[41] composed, prescribed, or laid down

[42] George Buchanan, in *The Powers of the Crown in Scotland* (1579), argues that Samuel was a legitimate ruler appointed by God and that in rejecting their covenant with Samuel in order to be ruled by tyrants, the people of Israel were rejecting God: "Samuel had judged them lawfully, according to the principles of the divine laws. But when, in his old age, his sons judged in his stead, they did many things that were wrong and delivered judgments contrary to the laws. Now I can see no reason why the people should have asked for a change in the form of government in preference to asking that the faults of the one they had should be corrected .... They asked for a king, such as the neighboring nations had, who

Scripture, being well understood, is so pertinent for our purpose, I have insert[ed] herein the very words of the text.

> 9 Now therefore hearken to their voice, howbeit[43] yet testify unto them and show them the manner of the king that shall reign over them.
> 10 So Samuel told all the words of the Lord unto the people that asked a king of him.
> 11 And he said, "This shall be the manner of the king that shall reign over you: he will take your sons, and appoint them to his charets,[44] and to be his horsemen, and some shall run before his charet.
> 12 "Also, he will make them his captains over thousands, and captains over fifties, and to ear[45] his ground, and to reap his harvest, and to make instruments of war, and the things that serve for his charets.
> 13 "He will also take your daughters and make them apothecaries, and cooks, and bakers.
> 14 "And he will take your fields, and your vineyards, and your best olive trees, and give them to his servants.
> 15 "And he will take the tenth of your seed, and of your vineyards, and give it to his eunuchs, and to his servants.
> 16 "And he will take your menservants, and your maidservants, and the chief of your young men, and your asses, and put them to his work.
> 17 "He will take the tenth of your sheep, and ye shall be his servants.
> 18 "And ye shall cry out at that day because of your king, whom ye have chosen you; and the Lord God will not hear you at that day."
> 19 But the people would not hear the voice of Samuel, but did say: "Nay, but there shall be a king over us.
> 20 "And we also will be like all other nations, and our king shall judge us, and go out before us, and fight our battles."[46]

That these words and discourses of Samuel were dited by God's spirit it needs no further probation but that it is a place of Scripture, since the whole Scripture is dited by that inspiration, as Paul saith,[47] which ground no good Christian will, or dare, deny. Whereupon it must necessarily follow that these speeches proceeded not from any

---

would be a judge at home and a military commander against outside foes. But these kings were, in effect tyrants" (111).

[43] nevertheless

[44] war-chariots

[45] to plough

[46] 1 Samuel 8:9–20

[47] See 2 Timothy 3:16: "All scripture is given by inspiration of God, and is profitable for doctrine, for reproof, for correction, for instruction in righteousness." James may also have been thinking of 1 Corinthians 1–4, in which Paul makes an extended argument about divine inspiration.

ambition in Samuel, as one loath to quit the reins that he so long had ruled and therefore desirous, by making odious the government of a king, to dissuade the people from their farther importunate craving of one. For as the text proveth it plainly, he then convened them to give them a resolute grant of their demand, as God by his own mouth commanded him, saying, "Hearken to the voice of the people."[48] And to press to dissuade them from that which he then came to grant unto them were a thing very impertinent in a wise man, much more in the prophet of the most high God. And likewise it well appeared in all the course of his life after, that his so long refusing of their suit before came not of any ambition in him, which he well proved in praying and, as it were, importuning God for the weal of Saul. Yea, after God had declared his reprobation unto him, yet he desisted not, while God himself was wrath at his praying, and discharged his father's suit in that errand.[49]

And that these words of Samuel were not uttered as a prophesy of Saul their first king's defection, it well appeareth as well because we hear no mention made in the Scripture of any [of] his tyranny and oppression (which, if it had been, would not have been left un-painted out therein, as well as his other faults were, as in a true mirror of all the king's behaviours, whom it describeth), as likewise in respect that Saul was chosen by God for his virtue and meet[50] qualities to govern his people, whereas his defection sprung after-hand from the corruption of his own nature and not through any default in God, whom they that think so would make as a stepfather to his people in making willfully a choice of the unmeetest for

---

[48] James seems to be citing and conflating 1 Samuel 8:7: "And the Lord said unto Samuel, Hearken unto the voice of the people in all that they say unto thee" and 1 Samuel 8:9: "Now therefore hearken unto their voice." The same chapter from Samuel ends with verses 21 and 22: "And Samuel heard all the words of the people, and he rehearsed them in the ears of the Lord. And the Lord said to Samuel, Hearken unto their voice, and make them a king. And Samuel said unto the men of Israel, Go ye every man unto his city." The passage is typical of the rhetorical strategy used by James, on the one hand developing a notion of the people's voice, but finally asserting the necessity of the people's "due obedience" to the king.

[49] Saul was chosen by God and anointed by Samuel as the first king of the tribes of Israel. James is arguing that Samuel was not motivated by ambition because he continued to pray on Saul's behalf after God had rejected him for his failure to destroy the Amalekites (see 1 Samuel 16:1; also 1 Samuel 9–31 and 1 Chronicles 10). The 1598 version has this phrase as "while God himself was wrath at his praying, and discharged his farther suit in that errand" (*Minor Prose* 64; modernized). The 1616 version is almost certainly corrupt in this instance.

[50] appropriate

governing them, since the election of that king lay absolutely and immediately in God's hand. But by the contrary, it is plain and evident that this speech of Samuel to the people was to prepare their hearts before the hand to the due obedience of that king which God was to give unto them, and therefore opened up unto them what might be the intolerable qualities that might fall in some of their kings, thereby preparing them to patience not to resist to God's ordinance, but as he would have said: "Since God hath granted your importunate suit in giving you a king, as ye have else committed an error in shaking off God's yoke and over-hasty seeking of a king, so beware ye fall not into the next in casting off also rashly that yoke which God at your earnest suit hath laid upon you, how hard that ever it seem to be. For as ye could not have obtained one without the permission and ordinance of God, so may ye no more fro[51] he be once set over you shake him off without the same warrant. And therefore, in time arm yourselves with patience and humility, since he that hath the only power to make him hath the only power to unmake him, and ye only to obey, bearing with these straits[52] that I now foreshow you as with the finger of God, which lieth not in you to take off."

And will ye consider the very words of the text in order as they are set down, it shall plainly declare the obedience that the people owe to their king in all respects.[53]

First, God commandeth Samuel to do two things: the one, to grant the people their suit in giving them a king; the other, to forewarn them what some kings will do unto them, that they may not thereafter in their grudging and murmuring say, when they shall feel the snares[54] here forespoken: "We would never have had a king of God in case when we craved him he had let us know how we would have been used by him, as now we find but over-late." And this is meant by these words: "Now therefore hearken unto their voice, howbeit yet testify unto them and show them the manner of the king that shall rule over them."

---

[51] from the moment when

[52] hardships

[53] James, in succeeding paragraphs, provides a close reading of the citation from 1 Samuel 8:9–20. The passage is exemplary of James's use of exegesis as a tool for representing and authorizing his political power.

[54] This is possibly a printer's mistake in the 1616 version. The 1598 version uses the word "smartes," as in a sharp bodily or mental pain. There is a possibility that James is using "snares" in the sense of a device for tempting the enemy or dupe to expose himself to capture, defeat, or failure.

And next, Samuel, in execution of this commandment of God, he likewise doeth two things.

First, he declares unto them what points of justice and equity their king will break in his behaviour unto them. And next he putteth them out of hope that, weary as they will, they shall not have leave to shake off that yoke which God through their importunity hath laid upon them. The points of equity that the king shall break unto them are expressed in these words:

11 "He will take your sons and appoint them to his charets, and to be his horsemen, and some shall run before his charet.
12 "Also he will make them his captains over thousands, and captains over fifties, and to ear his ground, and to reap his harvest, and to make instruments of war, and the things that serve for his charets.
13 "He will also take your daughters and make them apothecaries, and cooks, and bakers."

The points of justice that he shall break unto them are expressed in these words:

14 "He will take your fields, and your vineyards, and your best olive trees, and give them to his servants.
15 "And he will take the tenth of your seed, and of your vineyards, and give it to his eunuchs, and to his servants, and also the tenth of your sheep."

As if he would say: "The best and noblest of your blood shall be compelled in slavish and servile offices to serve him and, not content of his own patrimony, will make up a rent to his own use out of your best lands, vineyards, orchards, and store of cattle; so as, inverting the law of nature and office of a king, your persons and the persons of your posterity together with your lands and all that ye possess shall serve his private use and inordinate appetite."

And as unto the next point (which is his forewarning them that, weary as they will, they shall not have leave to shake off the yoke which God through their importunity hath laid upon them), it is expressed in these words: "And ye shall cry out at that day because of your king whom ye have chosen you; and the Lord will not hear you at that day."

As he would say: "When ye shall find these things in proof that now I forewarn you of, although you shall grudge and murmur, yet it shall not be lawful to you to cast it off, in respect it is not only the ordinance of God but also yourselves have chosen him unto you, thereby renouncing forever all privileges by your willing consent out of your hands, whereby in any time hereafter ye would claim and call back unto yourselves again that power, which God shall not permit you to do." And for further taking away of all excuse and retraction of this their contract, after their consent to underlie this yoke with all the burdens that he hath declared unto them, he craves their answer and consent to his proposition, which appeareth by their answer as it is expressed in these words:

19 "Nay, but there shall be a king over us.
20 "And we also will be like all other nations, and our king shall judge us, and go out before us, and fight our battles."

As if they would have said: "All your speeches and hard conditions shall not scare us, but we will take the good and evil of it upon us, and we will be content to bear whatsoever burden it shall please our king to lay upon us as well as other nations do. And for the good we will get of him in fighting our battles, we will more patiently bear any burden that shall please him to lay on us."

Now then, since the erection of this kingdom and monarchy among the Jews and the law thereof may and ought to be a pattern to all Christian and well-founded monarchies, as being founded by God himself, who by his oracle and out of his own mouth gave the law thereof, what liberty can broiling spirits and rebellious minds claim justly to against any Christian monarchy, since they can claim to no greater liberty on their part nor the people of God might have done, and no greater tyranny was ever executed by any prince or tyrant whom they can object nor was here forewarned to the people of God (and yet all rebellion countermanded unto them), if tyrannizing over men's persons, sons, daughters, and servants, redacting[55] noble houses and men and women of noble blood to slavish and servile offices, and extortion and spoil of their lands and goods to the prince's own private use and commodity, and of his courtiers and servants, may be called a tyranny?[56]

---

[55] reducing

[56] The complexity of the syntax and the slipperiness of the rhetorical strategies in this single-sentence paragraph conceal a rather straightforward bit of thinking on the divine right of monarchs: if God authorizes kingship for the Jews, his chosen people, how can "rebellious minds" who claim that a particular Christian monarchy is a tyranny, expect any "greater liberty" from God, who authorizes the very notion of kingship and allowed tyranny over the Jews?

And that this proposition, grounded upon the Scripture, may the more clearly appear to be true by the practice oft-proved in the same book, we never read that ever the prophets persuaded the people to rebel against the prince, how wicked soever he was.

When Samuel, by God's command, pronounced to the same king Saul that his kingdom was rent from him and given to another (which in effect was a degrading of him), yet his next action following that was peacably to turn home and with floods of tears to pray to God to have some compassion upon him.[57]

And David,[58] notwithstanding he was inaugurate[d] in that same degraded king's room,[59] not only (when he was cruelly persecuted for no offence but good service done unto him) would not presume, having him in his power, skantly[60] but with great reverence to touch the garment of the anointed of the Lord[61] and in his words blessed him, but likewise when one came to him vaunting himself untruly to have slain Saul, he, without form of process or trial of his guilt, caused only for guiltiness of his tongue, put him to sudden death.[62]

And although there was never a more monstrous persecutor and tyrant nor Ahab was, yet all the rebellion that Elijah[63] ever raised against him was to fly to the wilderness, where, for fault of sustentation,[64] he was fed with the corbies.[65] And I think no man will doubt

---

[57]See 1 Samuel 15.

[58]See 1 Samuel 16–31; 2 Samuel; 1 Kings 1–2; and 1 Chronicles 10–29.

[59]place, position of authority

[60]scarcely

[61]Here James refers to 1 Samuel 24:1–8, which tells how David could have assassinated Saul in the cave of En-ged, but did not.

[62]See 2 Samuel 1:1–16.

[63]Ahab was king of Israel c. 873–853 BCE. He is famous for taking a foreigner as wife, Jezebel, and for allowing the worship of Baal, a fertility god, all of which brought him the censure of the prophet Elijah. See 1 Kings 16–22, and 2 Chronicles 18, 22. Buchanan argues that the murder of Ahab shows that the killing of tyrants is done at God's command: "the slaying of Ahab was done at God's command; and ... a reward was promised and paid to the killer, also by divine command. And so, should you appeal to the argument that all tyrants must be obeyed because God, through his prophet, in one instance ordered his people to obey a tyrant, you will immediately be told in reply that all tyrants should be put to death, because Ahab, at God's command, was destroyed by one of the officers of his own army" (117). Elijah was a prophet of the ninth century BCE who defended the Hebrew religion, particularly against the cult of Baal, brought into Israel by Ahab's wife, Jezebel. To escape the wrath of Jezebel, Elijah fled to Beer-sheba and into the desert. See 1 Kings 17–19, 21; 2 Kings 1; 2 Chronicles 21.

[64]The action of maintaining a person or thing in being or activity, or of keeping it from failing or perishing; especially in the seventeenth century, divine support.

[65]ravens; see 1 Kings 17:1–7 for a description of Elijah's three year sojourn by

but Samuel, David, and Elijah had as great power to persuade the people, if they had liked to have employed their credit, to uproars and rebellions against these wicked kings as any of our seditious preachers in these days of whatsoever religion, either in this country or in France, had that busied themselves most to stir up rebellion under cloak of religion. This far the only love of verity, I protest, without hatred at their persons, ha[s][66] moved me to be somewhat satiric.

And if any will lean to the extraordinary examples of degrading or killing of kings in the Scriptures thereby to cloak the people's rebellion, as by the deed of Jehu[67] and suchlike extraordinaries, I answer, besides that they want the like warrant that they had, if extraordinary examples of the Scripture shall be drawn in daily practice, murder under traist,[68] as in the persons of Ehud[69] and Jael;[70] theft, as in the persons of the Israelites coming out of Egypt;[71] lying to their parents to the hurt of their brother, as in the person of Jacob,[72] shall all be

---

the brook Cherith.

[66] "have" in original

[67] See 2 Kings 9–11. Jehu was King of Israel. He was a general for Ahab and after Ahab's death led a successful rebellion against Ahab's descendants, killing Ahab's widow, Jezebel, all his sons, and all the worshippers of the false god Baal. He is famous for his policy of total annihilation of the enemy represented by Baalism. Thereafter he founded the longest-lived dynasty in Israel's history, lasting four generations after his own rule of twenty-eight years.

[68] (committed under) trust

[69] See Judges 3:15–26 for the story of Ehud; also 1 Chronicles 7:10 and 8:6. The Israelites had been subjected by Eglon, king of Moab, and Ehud was chosen to free them by assassinating Eglon. James uses Ehud as an example of breach of the trust and hospitality shown by a sovereign to a subject.

[70] See Judges 4:15–21. Jael murdered Sisera, captain of the forces of Jabin, king of Canaan, who had subjugated the Israelites after the death of Ehud. When Sisera was defeated by Barak he fled to Jael's tent and was assured of his safety. After he had fallen asleep Jael took a tent peg and drove it through his head. Like the story of Ehud, James was interested in the concept of being murdered by somebody to whom you had given yourself in trust.

[71] Exodus 3:15, 21–22 and 12:33–36 mention the Israelites "spoil[ing]," as in despoiling, the Egyptians of their silver, gold, and raiment. As is his wont, James develops a politically expedient reading of a Scriptural passage to service his argument.

[72] See Genesis 25–37, 42–50. James may be referring to Jacob's famous deceit of his father, Isaac, with the help of his mother, Rebecca. Jacob (i. e., Israel) and Esau were twins who fought in the womb, Jacob being born holding on to Esau's foot. Jacob was the younger of the twins and his mother's favourite, Esau his father's favourite. When Isaac was blind and near death he sent Esau to hunt for meat to make a stew in order that he could bless Esau before he died. Rebecca overheard and told Jacob to counterfeit Esau by killing a kid and making a similar

counted as lawful and allowable virtues as rebellion against princes. And to conclude, the practice through the whole Scripture proveth the people's obedience given to that sentence in the law of God: "Thou shalt not rail upon the judges, neither speak evil of the ruler of thy people."[73]

To end, then, the ground of my proposition taken out of the Scripture, let two special and notable examples, one under the law, another under the evangel,[74] conclude this part of my allegiance. Under the law Jeremiah threateneth the people of God with utter destruction for rebellion to Nebuchadnezzar, the king of Babel,[75] who although he was an idolatrous persecutor, a foreign king, a tyrant and usurper of their liberties, yet in respect they had once received and acknowledged him for their king, he not only commandeth them to obey him but even to pray for his prosperity, adjoining the reason to it because in his prosperity stood their peace.[76]

---

stew for Isaac. The ruse worked and Jacob received Isaac's blessing. The incident would have had particular significance for James as it deals primarily with the right of primogeniture.

[73]James seems to have been thinking of the latter part of this quotation in regard to his own position as monarch. This may account for the obscurity of the first part of the passage, which does not occur in the Authorized King James Version of the Bible, but does occur in the Bassandyne and the Geneva Bibles (the former being the first Bible printed in Scotland [1579], though Robert Lekpreuik had been given a licence to print the Geneva Bible [1560] in 1568; the Bassandyne, likely the Bible used by James in the composition of *The True Law*, is so-named after its printer Thomas Bassandyne and is based on the Geneva version) in Exodus 22:28: "Thou shalt not rail upon the judges, neither speak evil of the ruler of thy people." The second part of James's citation may also be derived from Acts 23:5: "Thou shalt not speak evil of the ruler of thy people." James had clearly read the Bassandyne Bible carefully, for in preparing the 1611 Authorized Version he had made notations regarding specific passages and their interpretation. William T. Dobson comments on two of the verses that James objected to from the Bassandyne Bible, because they were "very partial, untrue, seditious, and savoring too much of dangerous and traitorous deceits" (140).

[74]the gospel; any of the four Gospels; a doctrine or principle (of politics and so forth); see also the OED's note that "In England the word was in [the] 17c. already archaic and purely literary, but in Scotland it remained in current use, as a synonym for *gospel*, until a still later period." James seems to be using "evangel" in its archaic sense as a referent for the principle of authority embodied in Scripture as the word of God.

[75]Babylon

[76]See Jeremiah 27:6–8 and Jeremiah 29. Nebuchadnezzar was king of Babylon during the last Babylonian empire and conquered Jerusalem in 597 BCE. James uses him as an example of the necessity of obeying even a foreign tyrant "because

And under the evangel, that king whom Paul bids the Romans "obey" and serve "for conscience's sake"[77] was Nero,[78] that bloody tyrant, an infamy to his age, and a monster to the world, being also an idolatrous persecutor as the king of Babel was. If, then, idolatry and defection from God, tyranny over their people, and persecution of the saints for their profession's sake hindered not the spirit of God to command his people under all highest pain to give them all due and hearty obedience for conscience's sake, giving to Caesar that which was Caesar's and to God that which was God's, as Christ saith,[79] and that this practice throughout the book of God agreeth with this law, which he made in the erection of that monarchy (as is at length before deduced), what shameless presumption is it to any Christian people nowadays to claim to that unlawful liberty which God refused to his own peculiar and chosen people? Shortly then, to take up in two or three sentences grounded upon all these arguments, out of the law of God, the duty and allegiance of the people to their lawful king, their obedience, I say, ought to be to him as to God's lieutenant in earth, obeying his commands in all things except directly against God as the commands of God's minister, acknowledging him a judge set by God over them, having power to judge them but to be judged only by God, whom to only he must give count of his judgement, fearing him as their judge, loving him as their father, praying for him as their protector, for his continuance, if he be good, for his amendment, if he be wicked, following and obeying his lawful commands, eschewing and flying his fury in his unlawful, without resistance but by sobs and tears to God according to that sentence

---

in his prosperity stood their peace." The argument has resonances with James's anxiety about his own position as a foreign king come to power in England.

[77] James may have been thinking of Romans 13:4–5: "For he is the minister of God to thee for good. But if thou do that which is evil, be afraid; for he beareth not the sword in vain: for he is the minister of God, a revenger to execute wrath upon him that doeth evil. Wherefore ye must needs be subject, not only for wrath, but also for conscience sake." The thirteenth chapter of Romans begins, interestingly enough in light of James's arguments about submission to sovereign authority, with the admonition "Let every soul be subject unto the higher powers" (Romans 13:1). A marginal note in the 1616 version also suggests Jeremiah 13 as a source or possible context for this passage.

[78] Nero was the Roman emperor from CE 54–68.

[79] See Matthew 22:21 and Mark 12:17. Christ answers this in response to the question "Is it lawful to give tribute to Caesar, or not?" (Mark 12:14; see also Matthew 22:17).

"The true picture of one Picte." From *A Briefe and True Report of the New Found Land of Virginia,* by Thomas Harriot (1590), translated by Richard Hakluyt. Engravings by Theodor de Bry based on drawings by John White and Jacques Le Moyne de Morgues.

used in the primitive church[80] in the time of the persecution, *preces et lacrimae sunt arma ecclesiae.*[81]

Now as for the describing the allegiance that the lieges owe to their native king out of the fundamental and civil law, especially of this country,[82] as I promised, the ground must first be set down of the first manner of establishing the laws and form of government among us, that the ground being first right laid, we may thereafter build rightly thereupon. Although it be true (according to the affirmation of those that pride themselves to be the scourges of tyrants) that in the first beginning of kings rising among Gentiles in the time of the first age, divers commonwealths and societies of men choosed out one among themselves who, for his virtues and valour being more eminent than the rest, was chosen out by them and set up in that room to maintain the weakest in their right, to throw down oppressors, and to foster and continue the society among men, which could not otherwise but by virtue of that unity be well done, yet these examples are nothing pertinent to us, because our kingdom and divers other monarchies are not in that case but had their beginning in a far contrary fashion.

For as our chronicles bear witness,[83] this isle, and especially our part of it, being scantly inhabited but by very few, and they as

---

[80] the Christian Church in its earliest and (by implication) purest times

[81] prayers and tears are the weapons of the church; New Testament persecution refers to persecution of the church by Jewish opponents or by Roman authorities, the latter category falling into three periods: before the Neronian persecution, the Neronian persecution, and persecutions under the Flavian dynasty (CE 69–96, during which the emperor Vespasian and his sons Titus and Domitian ruled).

[82] Scotland has a civil law system based on principles from Roman law, as opposed to England's reliance on a common law of tradition and precedent. James's reliance upon civil law marks a difference in his legal thinking from the stress upon common law that he was to encounter in his move to England. Civil law, as a set of statutes alterable by royal prerogative, was in England "associated with arbitrary government" (Kevin Sharpe, *Politics and Ideas in Early Stuart England* 175), as opposed to common law, thought of—with some reservations—as a set of unalterable precepts binding on both monarch and people. See Sharpe, 174–81.

[83] James had in his library a copy of Hector Boethius's 1527 *Historia Scotorum* (published in Scots English as *Chronicle of Scotland* [1540?], reprinted in Amsterdam by Theatrum Orbis Terrarum, 1977). Boethius's account is somewhat different in emphasis than James's. The Scots, fearing invasion by both the Picts (an ancient people who once inhabited parts of northern Britain before assimilating with the Scots) and the Britons, decide in council to call on the Irish for help and to choose one to rule over the others in order to avoid sedition in the time of crisis. Ferquhard, "king of Scots in Ireland," sends his son Fergus to aid the Scots. In a second council the Scots decide to have one king rule over

barbarous and scant of civility as number, there comes our first king
Fergus with a great number with him out of Ireland, which was long
inhabited before us, and making himself master of the country by his
own friendship and force, as well of the Ireland-men that came with
him as of the countrymen that willingly fell to him, he made himself
king and lord as well of the whole lands as of the whole inhabitants
within the same. Thereafter he and his successors, a long while after
their being kings, made and established their laws from time to time
and as the occasion required. So the truth is directly contrary in our
state to the false affirmation of such seditious writers as would
persuade us that the laws and state of our country were established
before the admitting of a king,[84] where, by the contrary, ye see it
plainly proved that a wise king, coming in among barbars,[85] first
established the estate and form of government and thereafter made
laws by himself and his successors according thereto.

The kings, therefore, in Scotland were before any estates or ranks
of men within the same, before any Parliaments were holden or laws
made; and by them was the land distributed (which at the first was
whole theirs), states erected and decerned,[86] and forms of government devised and established. And so it follows of necessity that the
kings were the authors and makers of the laws, and not the laws of
the kings. And to prove this my assertion more clearly, it is evident
by the roles of our chancellery[87] (which contain our eldest and
fundamental laws) that the king is *dominus omnium bonorum* and
dominus directus totius dominii,[88] the whole subjects being but his

---

them in peace as well as war, and they choose Fergus in order to avoid the
competition and strife that would ensue if they chose a Scot. Fergus manages to
band with the Picts and defeat the Britons. By general consent, there is a partition
of the lands among Fergus's captains, and the people choose seven prudent men
to work out the divisions. The people agree to be ruled by one king, and Fergus
and his successors are given charter to rule. There is, obviously, more
consultation, agreement, and consent—and consequently less
conquest—involved here than James indicates.

[84]For instance, Buchanan refers to the chronicles to help him argue that
Scotland has always had a government of law, that kings in Scotland have
traditionally been held accountable to the law for their actions, and that Scotland
is a limited and not an absolute monarchy (100–107).

[85]barbarians

[86]delimited

[87]The chancellery, or chancery, is the office of the chancellor, head of the king's
council and the crown's chief legal authority. The chancellery is responsible for
issuing legal writs, such as charters and warrants, in the king's name.

[88]These are ideas from Roman law. In this context *dominus* means owner;
bona is the whole of an individual's property. *Dominus omnium bonorum* means

vassals and from him holding all their lands as their overlord, who, according to good services done unto him, changes their holdings from tack to few, from ward to blanch,[89] erecteth new baronies and uniteth old, without advice or authority of either Parliament or any other subaltern judicial seat. So as if wrong might be admitted in play (albeit I grant wrong should be wrong in all persons), the king might have a better colour for his pleasure without further reason to take the land from his lieges as overlord of the whole and do with it as pleaseth him, since all that they hold is of him, than as foolish writers say, the people might unmake the king and put another in his room.[90] But either of them, as unlawful and against the ordinance of God, ought to be alike odious to be thought, much less put in practice.

And according to these fundamental laws already alleged, we daily see that in the Parliament (which is nothing else but the head court of the king and his vassals)[91] the laws are but craved by his subjects and only made by him at their rogation[92] and with their advice. For albeit the king make daily statutes and ordinances,

---

owner of everybody's property. *Dominium directum* is the nominal right of ownership remaining with an owner who has granted exclusive right of enjoyment over a thing to another. Roman law distinguishes between the owner *(dominus)* and the *possessor* (see Adolf Berger, *Encyclopedic Dictionary of Roman Law* [Philadelphia: American Philosophical Society, 1953]). James appears to be arguing that he is the owner of all the property of which others are only the possessors. *Dominus directus totius dominii* means "the ultimate owner of all ownership." Jonathan Goldberg argues for the importance of Roman law in James's thought (see *James I and the Politics of Literature* 117ff, 264–265n8).

[89]James is enumerating various relations between landowner and tenant: tack is leasehold tenure; few is perpetual lease for a fixed rent; ward holding is tenure by military service or a payment in commutation of military service; blanch holding is rent paid in silver instead of service, labour, or produce.

[90]Buchanan, for instance, argues that there are grounds upon which a king may be rightfully and lawfully deposed (102–104).

[91]James's conception of Parliament, as expressed here, was too simplistic to deal with the Parliament that he was to encounter on his move to England. For an account of the complexity and contentiousness within Parliament and between king and Parliament in early Stuart England, see Barry Coward, *The Stuart Age: A History of England 1603–1714* (London: Longman, 1980), 88–91, 114–23. Although the English Parliament agreed in large measure with James's conception of his power and prerogatives, it was wary of encroachments on its place in governmental practice, rife with tension between various local interests, and capable of uniting in principle against the king on particularly sensitive issues. James's relations with the English Parliament bear similarities to the conflictual relation with the kirk in which he often found himself while in Scotland.

[92]act of submitting a law for acceptance

enjoining such pains thereto as he thinks meet, without any advice of Parliament or estates, yet it lies in the power of no Parliament to make any kind of law or statute without his scepter be to it, for giving it the force of a law. And although divers changes have been in other countries of the blood royal and kingly house, the kingdom being wrest[ed][93] by conquest from one to another, as in our neighbour country in England (which was never in ours), yet the same ground of the king's right over all the land and subjects thereof remaineth alike in all other free monarchies, as well as in this. For when the Bastard of Normandy came into England and made himself king,[94] was it not by force and with a mighty army? Where he gave the law and took none, changed the laws, inverted the order of government, set down the strangers, his followers, in many of the old possessors' rooms, as at this day well appeareth a great part of the gentlemen in England being come of the Norman blood, and their old laws, which to this day they are ruled by, are written in his language, and not in theirs. And yet his successors have with great happiness enjoyed the crown to this day, whereof the like was also done by all them that conquested them before.

And for conclusion of this point, that the king is overlord over the whole lands, it is likewise daily proved by the law of our hoards,[95] of want of heirs, and of bastardies. For, if a hoard be found under the earth, because it is no more in the keeping or use of any person, it of the law pertains to the king. If a person, inheritor of any lands or goods, die without any sort of heirs, all his lands and goods return to the king. And if a bastard die unrehabiled,[96] without heirs of his body (which rehabiling only lies in the king's hands), all that he hath likewise returns to the king. And as ye see it manifest that the king is overlord of the whole land, so is he master over every person that inhabiteth the same, having power over the life and death of every one of them. For although a just prince will not take the life of any of his subjects without a clear law, yet the same laws whereby he taketh them are made by himself or his predecessors; and so the power flows always from himself, as by daily experience we see good and just princes will from time to time make new laws and statutes, adjoining the penalties to the breakers thereof, which, before the law was made, had been no crime to the subject to have committed. Not

---

[93] "wrest" in original
[94] William the Conqueror invaded England in 1066.
[95] abandoned or buried treasure
[96] not legitimated

that I deny the old definition of a king and of a law, which makes the
king to be a speaking law and the law a dumb king;[97] for certainly a
king that governs not by his law can neither be countable to God for
his administration nor have a happy and established reign. For albeit
it be true that I have at length proved that the king is above the law,
as both the author and giver of strength thereto, yet a good king will
not only delight to rule his subjects by the law but even will conform
himself in his own actions thereunto, always keeping that ground
that the health of the commonwealth be his chief law. And where he
sees the law doubtsome[98] or rigorous, he may interpret or mitigate
the same, lest otherwise *summum jus* be *summa injuria.*[99] And
therefore general laws made publicly in Parliament may, upon
known respects to the king, by his authority be mitigated and suspended upon causes only known to him.

As likewise, although I have said a good king will frame all his
actions to be according to the law, yet is he not bound thereto but
of his good will and for good example-giving to his subjects. For as
in the law of abstaining from eating of flesh in Lenton,[100] the king will
for example's sake make his own house to observe the law, yet no
man will think he needs to take a licence to eat flesh. And although
by our laws the bearing and wearing of hagbuts[101] and pistolets be
forbidden, yet no man can find any fault in the king for causing his
train [to] use them in any raid upon the borderers or other malefactors
or rebellious subjects. So, as I have already said, a good king,
although he be above the law, will subject and frame his actions
thereto for example's sake to his subjects, and of his own free will,
but not as subject or bound thereto.

Since I have so clearly proved, then, out of the fundamental laws
and practice of this country, what right and power a king hath over
his land and subjects, it is easy to be understood what allegiance and
obedience his lieges owe unto him; I mean always of such free
monarchies as our king is, and not of elective kings, and much less
of such sort of governors as the dukes of Venice are, whose aristocratic and limited government is nothing like to free monarchies,
although the malice of some writers hath not been ashamed to
misknow any difference to be betwixt them.[102] And if it be not lawful

---

[97] Buchanan quotes Cicero (*De Legibus* 3.2) in this regard (58).
[98] doubtful
[99] highest justice; highest injustice
[100] Lent
[101] an early type of portable gun, an arquebus
[102] For an example of the argument James is attacking, that there is no great

to any particular lord's tenants or vassals, upon whatsoever pretext, to control and displace their master and overlord (as is clearer nor the sun by all laws of the world), how much less may the subjects and vassals of the great overlord, the king, control or displace him? And since, in all inferior judgements in the land, the people may not upon any respects displace their magistrates, although but subaltern: for the people of a borough cannot displace their provost[103] before the time of their election; nor in ecclesiastical policy the flock can upon any pretence displace the pastor nor judge of him; yea, even the poor schoolmaster cannot be displaced by his scholars; if these, I say (whereof some are but inferior, subaltern, and temporal magistrates, and none of them equal in any sort to the dignity of a king), cannot be displaced for any occasion or pretext by them that are ruled by them, how much less is it lawful upon any pretext to control or displace the great provost and great schoolmaster of the whole land? Except by inverting the order of all law and reason, the commanded may be made to command their commander, the judged to judge their judge, and they that are governed to govern their time about their lord and governor.

And the agreement of the law of nature in this our ground with the laws and constitutions of God and man already alleged will, by two similitudes, easily appear. The king towards his people is rightly compared to a father of children and to a head of a body composed of divers members. For as fathers the good princes and magistrates of the people of God acknowledge themselves to their subjects. And for all other well-ruled commonwealths, the style of *pater patriae*[104] was ever, and is commonly, used to kings. And the proper office of a king towards his subjects agrees very well with the office of the head towards the body and all members thereof. For from the head, being the seat of judgement, proceedeth the care and foresight of guiding and preventing all evil that may come to the body or any part thereof. The head cares for the body; so doth the king for his people. As the discourse and direction flow from the head and the execution according thereunto belongs to the rest of the members, every one according to their office, so is it betwixt a wise prince and his people. As the judgement coming from the head may not only employ the members, every one in their own office, as long as they are able for

---

difference between a king, a duke, an emperor, or a consul, and that the Duke of Venice is a king under a constitutional government, see Buchanan, 56–57.

[103]Scottish equivalent of a mayor

[104]father of the fatherland

it, but likewise, in case any of them be affected with any infirmity, must care and provide for their remedy, in case it be curable, and, if otherwise, gar[105] cut them off for fear of infecting of the rest, even so is it betwixt the prince and his people. And as there is ever hope of curing any diseased member by the direction of the head, as long as it is whole, but, by the contrary, if it be troubled, all the members are partakers of that pain, so is it betwixt the prince and his people.[106]

And now, first for the father's part (whose natural love to his children I described in the first part of this my discourse, speaking of the duty that kings owe to their subjects), consider, I pray you, what duty his children owe to him and whether upon any pretext whatsoever it will not be thought monstrous and unnatural to his sons to rise up against him, to control him at their appetite, and, when they think good, to slay him or to cut him off and adopt to themselves any other they please in his room. Or can any pretence of wickedness or rigour on his part be a just excuse for his children to put hand into[107] him? And, although we see by the course of nature that love useth[108] to descend more than to ascend, in case it were true that the father hated and wronged the children never so much, will any man endued[109] with the least spunk[110] of reason think it lawful for them to meet him with the line?[111] Yea, suppose the father were furiously following his sons with a drawn sword, is it lawful for them to turn and strike again or make any resistance but by flight? I think surely, if there were no more but the example of brute beasts and unreasonable creatures, it may serve well enough to qualify and prove this my argument. We read often the piety that the storks have to their old and decayed parents. And generally we know that there are many sorts of beasts and fowls that with violence and many bloody strokes will beat and banish their young ones from them, how soon they perceive them to be able to fend themselves; but we never read or heard of any resistance on their part, except among the vipers, which proves such persons as ought to be reasonable creatures and yet

---

[105]cause to be done or to happen

[106]For a discussion of the prevalence in the political discourse of early modern England of analogies of father to children and head to body in the understanding of the relation of king to people, see Sharpe, 52–63.

[107]seize

[108]is accustomed to, tends

[109]endowed

[110]spark

[111]This is most likely a misprint. The edition of 1598 reads "meet him with the like." The Latin translation of 1604 reads "*par pari referre*": to repay in kind.

unnaturally follow this example to be endued with their viperous nature.

And for the similitude of the head and the body, it may very well fall out that the head will be forced to gar cut off some rotten member (as I have already said) to keep the rest of the body in integrity; but what state the body can be in if the head, for any infirmity that can fall to it, be cut off, I leave it to the reader's[112] judgement.

So as to conclude this part, if the children may, upon any pretext that can be imagined, lawfully rise up against their father, cut him off, and choose any other whom they please in his room, and if the body, for the weal of it, may, for any infirmity that can be in the head, strike it off, then I cannot deny that the people may rebel, control, and displace or cut off their king at their own pleasure and upon respects moving them. And whether these similitudes represent better the office of a king or the offices of masters, or deacons of crafts,[113] or doctors in physic (which jolly comparisons are used by such writers as maintain the contrary proposition),[114] I leave it also to the reader's discretion.

And in case any doubts might arise in any part of this treatise, I will (according to my promise) with the solution of four principal and most weighty doubts that the adversaries may object conclude this discourse. And first it is casten up by divers that employ their pens upon apologies for rebellions and treasons: that every man is born to carry such a natural zeal and duty to his commonwealth as to his mother; that, seeing it so rent[115] and deadly wounded as whiles it will be by wicked and tyrannous kings, good citizens will be forced, for the natural zeal and duty they owe to their own native country, to put their hand to work for freeing their commonwealth from such a pest.

Whereunto I give two answers. First, it is a sure axiom in theology that evil should not be done that good may come of it. The wicked-

---

[112] or possibly "readers'"

[113] principal officers of incorporated trades in Scottish towns

[114] For an example of the argument James is attacking, that the king is like a physician to the body politic, see Buchanan, 48ff. See also, paradoxically, the second book of *Basilikon Doron*, where James states: "And that ye may the readier with wisdom and justice govern your subjects by knowing what vices they are naturally most inclined to, as a good physician who must first know what peccant humours his patient naturally is most subject unto before he can begin his cure, I shall therefore shortly note unto you the principal faults that every rank of the people of this country is most affected unto."

[115] torn or pulled asunder

ness, therefore, of the king can never make them that are ordained to be judged by him to become his judges. And if it be not lawful to a private man to revenge his private injury upon his private adversary (since God hath only given the sword to the magistrate), how much less is it lawful to the people or any part of them (who all are but private men, the authority being always with the magistrate, as I have already proved) to take upon them the use of the sword, whom to it belongs not, against the public magistrate, whom to only it belongeth?

Next, in place of relieving the commonwealth out of distress (which is their only excuse and colour), they shall heap double distress and desolation upon it; and so their rebellion shall procure the contrary effects that they pretend it for. For a king cannot be imagined to be so unruly and tyrannous but the commonwealth will be kept in better order, notwithstanding thereof, by him than it can be by his way-taking.[116] For first, all sudden mutations are perilous in commonwealths, hope being thereby given to all bare[117] men to set up themselves and fly with other men's feathers, the reins being loosed to all the insolencies that disordered people can commit by hope of impunity, because of the looseness of all things.

And next, it is certain that a king can never be so monstrously vicious but he will generally favour justice and maintain some order, except in the particulars wherein his inordinate lusts and passions carry him away; where, by the contrary, no king being, nothing is unlawful to none. And so the old opinion of the philosophers proves true: that better it is to live in a commonwealth where nothing is lawful than where all things are lawful to all men, the commonwealth at that time resembling an undaunted[118] young horse that hath casten his rider. For as the divine poet Du Bartas saith, "Better it were to suffer some disorder in the estate and some spots in the commonwealth than, in pretending to reform, utterly to overthrow the republic."[119]

---

[116]Buchanan discusses the cases in which it is or is not advisable to depose a tyrant for the sake of the commonwealth (145–47).

[117]destitute, indigent

[118]untamed

[119]See Guillaume de Saluste, Seignieur Du Bartas, *La Seconde Sepmaine, Les Capitaines,* lines 1107–1110:

> Il vaut mieux supporter les jeunesses d'un roy,
> Quelque tache en l'estat, quelque vice en la loy,
> Que d'emplir tout le sang de vos effrois paniques,
> Et pensant reformer perdre les republiques.

The second objection they ground upon the curse that hangs over the commonwealth where a wicked king reigneth; and, say they, there cannot be a more acceptable deed in the sight of God, nor more dutiful to their commonweal, than to free the country of such a curse and vindicate to them their liberty, which is natural to all creatures to crave.[120]

Whereunto for answer, I grant, indeed, that a wicked king is sent by God for a curse to his people and a plague for their sins; but that it is lawful to them to shake off that curse at their own hand, which God hath laid on them, that I deny and may do so justly. Will any deny that the king of Babel was a curse to the people of God, as was plainly forespoken and threatened unto them in the prophecy of their captivity?[121] And what was Nero to the Christian church in his time? And yet Jeremiah and Paul (as ye have else[122] heard) commanded them not only to obey them but heartily to pray for their welfare.

It is certain, then (as I have already by the law of God sufficiently proved), that patience, earnest prayers to God, and amendment of their lives are the only lawful means to move God to relieve them of that heavy curse. As for vindicating to themselves their own liberty, what lawful power have they to revoke to themselves again those privileges which by their own consent before were so fully put out of their hands? For if a prince cannot justly bring back again to himself the privileges once bestowed by him or his predecessors upon any state or rank of his subjects, how much less may the subjects reave[123] out of the prince's hand that superiority which he and his predecessors have so long brooked over them?

(Better to put up with the immaturity of a king, some stain on the state, some vice in the law, than fill the blood with your panic-stricken fears, and thinking to reform, lose the republics.) The first part of *La Seconde Sepmaine* was published in 1584; the section containing *Les Capitaines* was not published until 1603. James entertained Du Bartas in Scotland in 1587 and most likely saw this work in manuscript. *La Seconde Sepmaine* deals with the events following the week in which God created the world. *Les Capitaines* ends with the events in 1 Samuel 8, which James has quoted at length, concerning the Israelites' desire to have a king. Du Bartas narrates a debate among the Israelites as to whether democratic, aristocratic, or monarchical rule is best. Du Bartas is even-handed in his judgements, but concludes that those born under a king should not strive to change the way they are governed. The lines James refers to come at this point in the poem as a caution against rebellion.

[120]Buchanan argues that it is a just and religious act to depose a tyrant (143–45).
[121]James is referring to 2 Kings 20:17, which prophesies the Babylonian captivity under Nebuchadnezzar.
[122]elsewhere
[123]pluck

But the unhappy iniquity of the time, which hath ofttimes given over good success to their treasonable attempts, furnisheth them the ground of their third objection: for, say they, the fortunate success that God hath so oft given to such enterprises proveth plainly by the practice that God favoured the justness of their quarrel.

To the which I answer, that it is true indeed that all the success of battles as well as other worldly things lieth only in God's hand; and therefore it is that in the Scripture he takes to himself the style of God of hosts. But upon that general to conclude that he ever gives victory to the just quarrel would prove the Philistines and divers other neighbour enemies of the people of God to have ofttimes had the just quarrel against the people of God, in respect of the many victories they obtained against them. And by that same argument, they had also just quarrel against the Ark of God, for they won it in the field and kept it long prisoner in their country.[124] As likewise by all good writers, as well theologues[125] as other, the duels and singular combats are disallowed, which are only made upon pretence that God will kithe[126] thereby the justice of the quarrel. For we must consider that the innocent party is not innocent before God, and therefore God will make ofttimes them that have the wrong side revenge justly his quarrel and when he hath done, cast his scourge in the fire, as he ofttimes did to his own people, stirring up and strengthening their enemies while they were humbled in his sight, and then delivered them in their hands. So God, as the great judge, may justly punish his deputy and for his rebellion against him stir up his rebels to meet him with the like. And when it is done, the part of the instrument is no better than the devil's part is in tempting and torturing such as God commiteth to him, as his hangman, to do. Therefore, as I said in the beginning, it is ofttimes a very deceivable argument to judge of the cause by the event.

And the last objection is grounded upon the mutual paction[127] and adstipulation[128] (as they call it) betwixt the king and his people at the

---

[124]The capture of the Ark of the Covenant by the Philistines is recounted in 1 Samuel 4–7; its recovery by David is recounted in 2 Samuel 6.

[125]theologians

[126]make known

[127]act of making a pact

[128]James seems to be misusing this term from Roman law. *Adstipulo* is a legal agreement in which a third party is brought in to promise on behalf of one of the two contracting parties. Here James seems to mean rather *stipulo*, which is simply a legal agreement between two parties (see W. W. Buckland, *A Text-Book of Roman Law from Augustus to Justinian*, rev. by Peter Stein, third ed. [Cambridge:

time of his coronation. For there, say they, there is a mutual paction and contract bound up and sworn betwixt the king and the people, whereupon it followeth that, if the one part of the contract or the indent[129] be broken upon the king's side, the people are no longer bound to keep their part of it but are thereby freed of their oath. For, say they, a contract betwixt two parties of all law frees the one party if the other break unto him.[130]

As to this contract alleged made at the coronation of a king: although I deny any such contract to be made then, especially containing such a clause irritant[131] as they allege, yet I confess that a king at his coronation, or at the entry to his kingdom, willingly promiseth to his people to discharge honourably and truly the office given him by God over them. But presuming that thereafter he break his promise unto them never so inexcusable, the question is who should be judge of the break, giving unto them this contract were made unto them never so sicker[132] according to their allegiance? I think no man that hath but the smallest entrance into the civil law will doubt that of all law, either civil or municipal of any nation, a contract cannot be thought broken by the one party, and so the other likewise to be freed therefrom, except that first a lawful trial and cognition[133] be had by the ordinary judge of the breakers thereof; or else every man may be both party and judge in his own cause, which is absurd once to be thought. Now in this contract, I say, betwixt the king and his people, God is doubtless the only judge, both because to him only the king must make count of his administration (as is oft said before) as likewise by the oath in the coronation God is made judge and revenger of the breakers. For in his presence, as only judge of oaths, all oaths ought to be made. Then, since God is the only judge betwixt the two parties contractors, the cognition and revenge must only appertain to him. It follows, therefore, of necessity that God must first give sentence upon the king that breaketh before the people can think themselves freed of their oath. What justice, then,

---

Cambridge UP, 1966], 436–45).

[129]indenture; formal agreement

[130]The infamous, anonymous French treatise of 1579, *Vindiciae contra Tyrannos* (*Legal Protections against Tyrants*), uses contract theory to defend resistance against tyrants and is a possible source for the position James is elaborating. See Sabine and Thorsen 352–57.

[131]a clause which sets out conditions which, if transgressed, render a contract null and void

[132]secure

[133]a judicial inquiry to establish the facts in a dispute

is it that the party shall be both judge and party, usurping upon himself the office of God, may by this argument easily appear.[134] And shall it lie in the hands of [the] headless multitude, when they please to weary of subjection, to cast off the yoke of government that God hath laid upon them; to judge and punish him whom by they should be judged and punished; and in that case wherein by their violence they kithe themselves to be most passionate parties to use the office of an ungracious judge or arbiter? Nay, to speak truly of that case as it stands betwixt the king and his people, none of them ought to judge of the other's break. For considering rightly the two parties at the time of their mutual promise, the king is the one party, and the whole people in one body are the other party. And therefore, since it is certain that a king, in case so it should fall out that his people in one body had rebelled against him, he should not in that case, as thinking himself free of his promise and oath, become an utter enemy and practice the wrack of his whole people and native country, although he ought justly to punish the principal authors and bellows of that universal rebellion. How much less, then, ought the people (that are always subject unto him and naked of all authority on their part) press to judge and overthrow him? Otherwise the people, as the one party contractors, shall no sooner challenge the king as breaker but he as soon shall judge them as breakers; so, as the victors making the tiners[135] the traitors (as our proverb is), the party shall aye become both judge and party in his own particular, as I have already said.

And it is here likewise to be noted that the duty and allegiance which the people sweareth to their prince is not only bound to themselves but likewise to their lawful heirs and posterity, the lineal succession of crowns being begun among the people of God and happily continued in divers Christian commonwealths; so as no objection, either of heresy or whatsoever private statute or law, may free the people from their oath-giving to their king and his succession, established by the old fundamental laws of the kingdom. For · as he is their heritable overlord and so by birth, not by any right in the coronation, cometh to his crown, it is alike unlawful (the crown ever standing full) to displace him that succeedeth thereto as to eject the former. For at the very moment of the expiring of the king

---

[134]Buchanan argues that the king can be held accountable to the law and the people and that there are Scottish precedents for the king to plead his case before judges (*The Powers of the Crown in Scotland* 131–32).

[135]losers

reigning, the nearest and lawful heir entereth in his place. And so to refuse him or intrude another is not to hold out uncoming in[136] but to expel and put out their righteous king. And I trust at this time whole[137] France acknowledgeth the superstitious rebellion of the leaguers[138] who, upon pretence of heresy, by force of arms held so long out, to the great desolation of their whole country, their native and righteous king from possessing of his own crown and natural kingdom.

Not that by all this former discourse of mine and apology for kings I mean that, whatsoever errors and intolerable abominations a sovereign prince commit, he ought to escape all punishment, as if thereby the world were only ordained for kings and they without controlment[139] to turn it upside down at their pleasure; but, by the contrary, by remitting them to God (who is their only ordinary judge), I remit them to the sorest and sharpest schoolmaster that can be devised for them. For the further a king is preferred by God above all other ranks and degrees of men, and the higher that his seat is above theirs, the greater is his obligation to his maker. And therefore, in case he forget himself (his unthankfulness being in the same measure of height), the sadder and sharper will his correction be; and according to the greatness of the height he is in, the weight of his fall will recompense the same. For the further that any person is obliged to God, his offence becomes and grows so much the greater than it would be in any other. Jove's thunderclaps light oftener and sorer upon the high and stately oaks than on the low and supple willow trees; and the highest bench is slidderiest[140] to sit upon. Neither is it ever heard that any king forgets himself towards God or in his vocation, but God, with the greatness of the plague, revengeth the greatness of his ingratitude. Neither think I by the force and argument of this my discourse so to persuade the people that none will hereafter be raised up and rebel against wicked princes. But remitting to the justice and providence of God to stir up such scourges as pleaseth him for punishment of wicked kings (who made

---

[136] refuse to grant admittance

[137] all of

[138] The Holy Union, or the Catholic League, formed in 1584, sought to keep the Protestant Henri of Navarre from the throne of France when the heir-apparent died without issue. The resultant civil war continued into the 1590s. James was, of course, very concerned that forces would league together to keep him from the English throne when Elizabeth died without children.

[139] restraint

[140] slipperiest

the very vermin and filthy dust of the earth to bridle the insolency of proud Pharaoh[141]), my only purpose and intention in this treatise is to persuade, as far as lieth in me, by these sure and infallible grounds, all such good Christian readers as bear not only the naked name of a Christian but kithe the fruits thereof in their daily form of life to keep their hearts and hands free from such monstrous and unnatural rebellions, whensoever the wickedness of a prince shall procure the same at God's hands; that, when it shall please God to cast such scourges of princes and instruments of his fury in the fire, ye may stand up with clean hands and unspotted consciences, having proved yourselves in all your actions true Christians toward God and dutiful subjects towards your king, having remitted the judgement and punishment of all his wrongs to him whom to only of right it appertaineth.

But craving at God and hoping that God shall continue his blessing with us in not sending such fearful desolation, I heartily wish our king's behaviour so to be, and continue among us, as our God in earth and loving father, endued with such properties as I described a king in the first part of this treatise; and that ye (my dear countrymen and charitable readers) may press by all means to procure the prosperity and welfare of your king, that, as he must on the one part think all his earthly felicity and happiness grounded upon your weal, caring more for himself for your sake than for his own, thinking himself only ordained for your weal, such holy and happy emulation may arise betwixt him and you as his care for your quietness and your care for his honour and preservation may in all your actions daily strive together; that the land may think themselves blessed with such a king, and the king may think himself most happy in ruling over so loving and obedient subjects.

---

[141] The plagues of frogs, lice, and flies are recounted in Exodus 8.

Basilikon Doron

Letters patent of James I investing his son Henry as Prince of
Wales and Earl of Chester (detail). By permission of
the British Library (Add Ms 36932).

Basilikon Doron:[1]
or
His Majesty's Instructions
To His Dearest Son, Henry the Prince

The Argument

Sonnet

> God gives not kings the style of gods in vain,[2]
> For on his throne his scepter do they sway;
> And as their subjects ought them to obey,
> So kings should fear and serve their God again.
> If, then, ye would enjoy a happy reign,
> Observe the statutes of your heavenly King,
> And from his law, make all your laws to spring.
> Since his lieutenant here ye should remain,
> Reward the just, be steadfast, true, and plain;
> Repress the proud,[3] maintaining aye[4] the right,
> Walk always so, as ever in his sight

---

[1]the king's gift, or the royal gift; in Greek letters in the original.

[2]James is referring to Psalm 82:6: "I have said, Ye *are* gods; and all of you *are* children of the most high." The context in which this passage occurs, however, is a criticism of injustice among the mighty and the judges. The following verse reads, "But ye shall die like men, and fall like one of the princes."

[3]James is referring to his motto, from Virgil's *Aeneid* 6.853: *"Parcere subjectis et debellare superbos"* (to spare the conquered and overthrow the proud).

[4]ever

Who guards the godly, plaguing the profane:
And so ye shall in princely virtues shine,
Resembling right your mighty King divine.[5]

To Henry, My Dearest Son and Natural Successor

Whom to can so rightly appertain this book of instructions to a prince in all the points of his calling, as well general, as a Christian towards God, as particular, as a king towards his people? Whom to, I say, can it so justly appertain as unto you, my dearest son? Since I, the author thereof, as your natural father, must be careful for your godly and virtuous education, as my eldest son and the first fruits of God's blessing towards me in my posterity, and as a king must timously[6] provide for your training up in all the points of a king's office, since ye are my natural and lawful successor therein, that, being rightly informed hereby of the weight of your burden, ye may in time begin to consider that, being born to be a king, ye are rather born to *onus* than *bonus*,[7] not excelling all your people so far in rank and honour as in daily care and hazardous painstaking for the dutiful administration of that great office that God hath laid upon your shoulders:

---

[5]The following sonnet, "The Dedication of the Book," appears only in the 1599 edition:

Lo here, my son, a mirror vive and fair,
Which showeth the shadow of a worthy king.
Lo here a book a pattern doth you bring,
Which ye should press to follow mair and mair.
This trusty friend the truth will never spare
But give a good advice unto you here:
How it should be your chief and princely care
To follow virtue, vice for to forbear.
And in this book your lesson will ye lear
For guiding of your people great and small;
Then, as ye ought, give an attentive ear
And panse how ye these precepts practice shall.
Your father bids you study here and read
How to become a perfect king indeed.

vive: life-like; mair: more; lear: learn; panse: consider

[6]early, opportunely

[7]*onus:* burden, responsibility; *bonus:* honour

laying so a just symmetry and proportion betwixt the height of your honourable place and the heavy weight of your great charge, and consequently, in case of failing, which God forbid, of the sadness of your fall according to the proportion of that height. I have, therefore, for the greater ease to your memory and that ye may at the first cast up any part that ye have to do with, divided this treatise in three parts. The first teacheth you your duty towards God as a Christian, the next your duty in your office as a king, and the third informeth you how to behave yourself in indifferent things, which of themselves are neither right nor wrong but according as they are rightly or wrongly used, and yet will serve, according to your behaviour therein, to augment or impair your fame and authority at the hands of your people. Receive and welcome this book, then, as a faithful preceptor[8] and counsellor unto you, which, because my affairs will not permit me ever to be present with you, I ordain to be a resident faithful admonisher of you. And because the hour of my death is uncertain to me as unto all flesh, I leave it as my testament and latter will unto you, charging you, in the presence of God and by the fatherly authority I have over you, that ye keep it ever with you as carefully as Alexander did the *Iliads* of Homer. Ye will find it a just and impartial counsellor, neither flattering you in any vice nor importuning you at unmeet[9] times. It will not come uncalled neither speak unspeered[10] at; and yet conferring with it when ye are at quiet, ye shall say with Scipio that ye are *"nunquam minus solus, quam cum solus."*[11] To conclude, then, I charge you, as ever ye think to deserve my fatherly blessing, to follow and put in practice, as far as lieth in you, the precepts hereafter following. And if ye follow the contrary course, I take the great God to record that this book shall one day be a witness betwixt me and you, and shall procure to be ratified in heaven the curse that in that case here I give unto you. For I protest before that great God I had rather not be a father, and childless, than be a father of wicked children. But hoping, yea, even promising unto myself, that God, who in his great blessing sent you unto me, shall in the same blessing as he hath given me a son so make him a good

---

[8]teacher, or book of instruction

[9]inappropriate

[10]unasked

[11]Never less alone than when alone, or alone with it (Cicero, *De Officiis* 3.1.1 and *De Republica* 1.17.27).

and a godly son, not repenting him of his mercy showed unto me, I end with my earnest prayer to God to work effectually into you the fruits of that blessing which here from my heart I bestow upon you.

Your loving father,

J. R.[12]

---

[12] *Jacobus Rex:* King James

To the Reader

Charitable reader, it is one of the golden sentences which Christ our Saviour uttered to his apostles that there is "nothing so covered that shall not be revealed, neither so hid that shall not be known; and whatsoever they have spoken in darkness should be heard in the light; and that which they had spoken in the ear in secret place should be publicly preached on the tops of the houses."[1] And since he hath said it, most true must it be, since the author thereof is the fountain and very being of truth: which should move all godly and honest men to be very wary in all their secretest actions and whatsoever middesses[2] they use for attaining to their most wished ends, lest, otherwise how avowable[3] soever the mark be whereat they aim, the middesses being discovered to be shameful whereby they climb, it may turn to the disgrace both of the good work itself and of the author thereof, since the deepest of our secrets cannot be hid from that all-seeing eye and penetrant[4] light, piercing through the bowels of very darkness itself.

But as this is generally true in the actions of all men, so is it more specially true in the affairs of kings; for kings, being public persons by reason of their office and authority, are, as it were, set (as it was said of old) upon a public stage in the sight of all the people,[5] where all the beholders' eyes are attentively bent to look and pry in the least circumstance of their secretest drifts:[6] which should make kings the

---

[1] Luke 12:2–3

[2] means

[3] approvable

[4] penetrating

[5] For an exposition of the lengthy intertextual history that lies behind this assertion, see Craigie's extensive note (*Basilikon Doron* 2.193–94).

[6] Goldberg, in *James I and the Politics of Literature,* makes much of this

more careful not to harbour the secretest thought in their mind, but such as in the[7] own time they shall not be ashamed openly to avouch, assuring themselves that Time, the mother of Verity, will in the due season bring her own daughter to perfection.

The true practice hereof I have as a king oft found in my own person, though, I thank God, never to my shame, having laid my count[8] ever to walk as in the eyes of the Almighty, examining ever so the secretest of my drifts before I gave them course as how they might someday bide the touchstone of a public trial. And amongst the rest of my secret actions which have (unlooked for of me) come to public knowledge, it hath so fared with my *Basilikon Doron*,[9] directed to my eldest son, which I wrote for exercise of mine own engine[10] and instruction of him who is appointed by God (I hope) to sit on my throne after me. For the purpose and matter thereof being only fit for a king, as teaching him his office, and the person whom for it was ordained a king's heir, whose secret counsellor and faithful admonisher it must be, I thought it no ways convenient nor comely that either it should to all be proclaimed, which to one only appertained (and especially being a messenger betwixt two so conjunct persons), or yet that the mould whereupon he should frame his future behaviour, when he comes both unto the perfection of his years and possession of his inheritance, should before the hand be made common to the people, the subject of his future happy government. And therefore, for the more secret and close keeping of them, I only permitted seven of them to be printed, the printer being first sworn for secrecy;[11] and these seven I dispersed amongst some of my trustiest servants to be kept closely by them, lest in case, by the iniquity or wearing of time, any of them might have been lost, yet some of them might have remained after me as witnesses to my son both of the honest integrity of my heart and of my fatherly affection and natural care towards him. But since, contrary to my intention and

---

passage as revealing a basic contradiction in James's discourse of monarchy: the king is both revealed, like an actor on a stage, and bound up in state secrecy (xii–xiv).

[7]its

[8]kept account of myself

[9]Greek letters in the original

[10]intellect

[11]On Waldegrave and the publication history of *Basilikon Doron*, see our Introduction and Editorial Note.

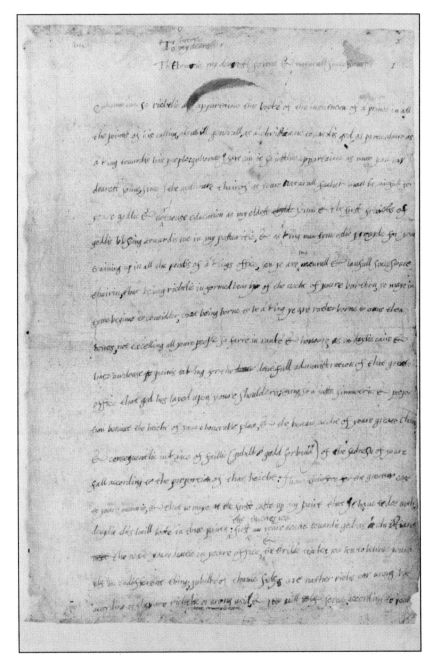

Opening page of the manuscript of *Basilikon Doron* in James's hand. By permission of the British Library (Royal Ms 18.B.IV).

expectation, as I have already said, this book is now vented[12] and set forth to the public view of the world and consequently subject to every man's censure as the current of his affection leads him, I am now forced, as well for resisting to the malice of the children of envy, who like wasps suck venom out of every wholesome herb, as for the satisfaction of the godly, honest sort in anything that they may mistake therein, both to publish and spread the true copies thereof for defacing of the false copies that are already spread, as I am informed, as likewise by this preface to clear such parts thereof as, in respect of the concised shortness of my style, may be misinterpreted therein.

To come, then, particularly to the matter of my book, there are two special, great points which (as I am informed) the malicious sort of men have detracted therein, and some of the honest sort have seemed a little to mistake: whereof the first and greatest is that some sentences therein should seem to furnish grounds to men to doubt of my sincerity in that religion which I have ever constantly professed;[13] the other is that in some parts thereof I should seem to nourish in my mind a vindictive resolution against England, or at the least some principals there, for the queen my mother's quarrel.[14]

The first calumny (most grievous indeed) is grounded upon the sharp and bitter words that therein are used in the description of the humours of Puritans[15] and rash-heady[16] preachers that think it their honour to contend with kings and perturb whole kingdoms. The other point is only grounded upon the straight charge I give my son not to hear nor suffer any unreverent speeches or books against any

---

[12]published

[13]As an infant, James was christened in the Catholic faith, but he was raised and educated in the reformed Church. Unlike radical reformers, however, he did not believe in the separation of church and state and wanted the church under state control. For this reason, he objected to anti-episcopal ideas among the reformers, thinking of the bishops and church hierarchy as a corollary and support of his own authority.

[14]Mary Queen of Scots was imprisoned in England from 1568 to 1587, at which time she was beheaded for her involvement in a plot to assassinate Elizabeth I.

[15]The term "Puritan" refers to a wide range of religious groups—Episcopalian, Presbyterian, Congregational, and Radical—who stood for simplification of ritual and freedom of worship from state interference. James uses the term in a much more limited sense, as outlined in the next paragraph.

[16]rash-headed

of his parents or progenitors, wherein I do allege my own experience anent[17] the queen my mother, affirming that I never found any that were of perfect age the time of her reign here so steadfastly true to me in all my troubles as these that constantly kept their allegiance to her in her time. But if the charitable reader will advisedly consider both the method and matter of my treatise, he will easily judge what wrong I have sustained by the carping at both. For my book, suppose very small, being divided in three several parts, the first part thereof only treats of a king's duty towards God in religion, wherein I have so clearly made profession of my religion, calling it the religion wherein I was brought up and ever made profession of, and wishing him ever to continue in the same as the only true form of God's worship, that I would have thought my sincere plainness in that first part upon that subject should have ditted[18] the mouth of the most envious Momus[19] that ever hell did hatch from barking at any other part of my book upon that ground, except they would allege me to be contrary to myself, which in so small a volume would smell of too great weakness and slipperiness of memory. And the second part of my book teaches my son how to use his office in the administration of justice and politic government; the third only containing a king's outward behaviour in indifferent things: what agreeance[20] and conformity he ought to keep betwixt his outward behaviour in these things and the virtuous qualities of his mind; and how they should serve for truchmen,[21] to interpret the inward disposition of the mind to the eyes of them that cannot see farther within him and therefore must only judge of him by the outward appearance. So as if there were no more to be looked into but the very method and order of the book, it will sufficiently clear me of that first and grievousest imputation in the point of religion: since in the first part, where religion is only treated of, I speak so plainly. And what in other parts I speak of Puritans, it is only of their moral faults, in that part where I speak of policy: declaring, when they contemn the law and sovereign authority, what exemplar punishment they deserve for the same. And now, as to the matter itself whereupon this scandal is

---

[17] concerning

[18] shut up

[19] Greek god of ridicule, a fault-finder

[20] agreement

[21] interpreters

taken: that I may sufficiently satisfy all honest men and by a just apology raise up a brazen wall or bulwark against all the darts of the envious, I will the more narrowly rip up the words whereat they seem to be somewhat stomached.[22]

First then, as to the name of Puritans: I am not ignorant that the style thereof doth properly belong only to that vile sect amongst the Anabaptists called the Family of Love because they think themselves only pure and in a manner without sin, the only true church, and only worthy to be participant of the sacraments, and all the rest of the world to be but abomination in the sight of God. Of this special sect I principally mean when I speak of Puritans, divers[23] of them, as Browne, Penry, and others,[24] having at sundry times come into Scotland to sow their popple[25] amongst us (and from my heart I wish

---

[22]offended, angered. The Scottish reformers were quick to take issue with whatever they took as attacks upon reformist positions—many of which might be associated with "Puritanism"; they were also quick to jump on anything in the king's behaviour which they took as "Papist," or Roman Catholic. After the publication of *Basilikon Doron,* for instance, Andrew Melville unsympathetically drew from it a set of "Anglo-pisco-papisticall Conclusiones"; it was attacks such as Melville's that forced James to write the present preface in defence of himself.

[23]various, sundry

[24]The Family of Love was the English offshoot of a Dutch sect founded by the mystic Hendrick Niclaes, who preached the attainability of spiritual perfection on earth. In his study, *The Family of Love in English Society, 1550–1630* (Cambridge: Cambridge UP, 1994), Christopher Marsh comments on this passage from *Basilikon Doron.* He notes that James's sweeping condemnations in the edition of 1599 had made English Puritans uneasy, and that by focussing his attack on a marginal and easily scapegoated group like the Familists, James successfully allayed the fears of English Puritans, "despite the rather obvious fact that when he spoke of 'puritans' throughout the remainder of the text, he quite clearly was not referring to the Family of Love" (200). M. M. Knappen writes, "In Elizabeth's reign the Anabaptists were more important as bogeymen than as a real political and religious force" (*Tudor Puritanism: A Chapter in the History of Idealism* [Gloucester, Massachusetts: Peter Smith, 1963], 372). Robert Browne (1550?–1663?) and John Penry (1559–1593) were Puritan separatists who advocated separation from the established Church and the founding of churches free from the control of the secular government. Browne visited Scotland from 1583 to 1584, Penry from 1589 to 1592. Like all Puritans, Browne and Penry denied "the royal right to compel beliefs or actions contrary to the Scripture" (Knappen 213).

[25]tares, weeds, especially metaphorical weeds sown by the devil. See Matthew

that they had left no scholars behind them who by their fruits will in the own time be manifested); and partly indeed I give this style to such brain-sick and heady preachers, their disciples and followers, as, refusing to be called of that sect, yet participate too much with their humours in maintaining the above-mentioned errors: not only agreeing with the general rule of all Anabaptists in the contempt of the civil magistrate and in leaning to their own dreams and revelations but particularly with this sect in accounting all men profane that swear not to all their fantasies; in making for every particular question of the policy of the church as great commotion as if the article of the Trinity were called in controversy; in making the Scriptures to be ruled by their conscience and not their conscience by the Scripture; and he that denies the least iota of their grounds, "*sit tibi tànquam ethnicus et publicanus,*"[26] not worthy to enjoy the benefit of breathing, much less to participate with them of the sacraments; and before that any of their grounds be impugned, let king, people, law, and all be trod under foot; such holy wars are to be preferred to an ungodly peace; no, in such cases Christian princes are not only to be resisted unto but not to be prayed for, for prayer must come of faith, and it is revealed to their consciences that God will hear no prayer for such a prince. Judge then, Christian reader, if I wrong this sort of people in giving them the style of that sect whose errors they imitate; and since they are contented to wear their livery,[27] let them not be ashamed to borrow also their name. It is only of this kind of men that in this book I write so sharply, and whom I wish my son to punish in case they refuse to obey the law and will not cease to stir up a rebellion, whom against I have written the more bitterly in respect of divers famous libels and injurious speeches spread by some of them, not only dishonourably invective against all Christian princes but even reproachful to our profession and religion, in respect they are come out under colour thereof, and yet were never answered but by Papists, who generally meddle as well against them as the religion itself, whereby the scandal was rather doubled than

---

13:24–25: "The kingdom of heaven is likened unto a man which sowed good seed in his field: But while men slept, his enemy came and sowed tares among the wheat, and went away."

[26]Let him be unto thee as an heathen man and a publican (Matthew 18:17).

[27]distinctive clothing worn by members of a company or servants of a noble household

taken away. But on the other part, I protest upon mine honour I mean it not generally of all preachers or others that like better of the single form of policy in our church than of the many ceremonies in the Church of England; that are persuaded that their bishops smell of a papal supremacy; that the surplice, the cornered cap, and suchlike are the outward badges of popish errors.[28] No, I am so far from being contentious in these things (which for my own part I ever esteemed as indifferent) as I do equally love and honour the learned and grave men of either of these opinions. It can no ways become me to pronounce so lightly a sentence in so old a controversy. We all (God be praised) do agree in the grounds; and the bitterness of men upon such questions doth but trouble the peace of the church and gives advantage and entry to the Papists by our division. But towards them I only use this provision: that where the law is otherwise they may content themselves soberly and quietly with their own opinions, not resisting to the authority nor breaking the law of the country, neither, above all, stirring any rebellion or schism; but possessing their souls in peace, let them press by patience and well grounded reasons either to persuade all the rest to like of their judgements or, where they see better grounds on the other part, not to be ashamed peaceably to incline thereunto, laying aside all preoccupied[29] opinions.

And that this is the only meaning of my book, and not any coldness or crack in religion, that place doth plainly witness where, after I have spoken of the faults in our ecclesiastical estate, I exhort my son to be beneficial unto the good men of the ministry, praising God there that there is presently a sufficient number of good men of them in this kingdom; and yet are they all known to be against the form of the English church. Yea, so far I am in that place from admitting corruption in religion as I wish him in promoving[30] them to use such caution as may preserve their estate from creeping to corruption, ever using that form through the whole book wherever I speak of bad preachers: terming them some of the ministers and not ministers

---

[28]The surplice is a loose, full-length or upper-body garment worn by Catholic and Anglican priests; the cornered cap was a rather unornamental headpiece worn by Anglican priests as a reaction against excessive display. More radical reformers, including those in Scotland, wanted to remove all aspects of ornamental vesture (which they associated with the lavish displays of Catholicism) from the exercise of religious ceremony.

[29]biased

[30]encouraging

or ministry in general. And to conclude this point of religion, what indifferency of religion can Momus call that in me where, speaking of my son's marriage (in case it pleased God before that time to cut the thread of my life), I plainly forewarn him of the inconvenients[31] that were like to ensue in case he should marry any that be of a different profession in religion from him; notwithstanding that the number of princes professing our religion be so small as it is hard to foresee how he can be that way meetly matched according to his rank?

And as for the other point, that by some parts in this book it should appear that I do nourish in my mind a vindictive resolution against England or some principals there: it is surely more than wonderful unto me upon what grounds they can have gathered such conclusions.[32] For as upon the one part I neither by name nor description point out England in that part of my discourse, so upon the other I plainly bewray[33] my meaning to be of Scottish men, where I conclude that purpose in these terms: that the love I bear to my son hath moved me to be so plain in this argument; for so that I discharge my conscience to him in uttering the verity, I care not what any traitor or treason-allower do think of it. And Englishmen could not thereby be meant, since they could be no traitors where they ought no allegiance. I am not ignorant of a wise and princely apophthegm which the same queen of England uttered about the time of her own coronation.[34] But the drift of that discourse doth fully clear my intention, being only grounded upon that precept to my son that he should not permit any unreverent detracting of his predecessors, bringing in that purpose of my mother only for an example of my experience anent Scottishmen, without using any persuasion to him of revenge. For a king's giving of any fault the due style infers no reduction of the faulter's pardon. No, I am by a degree nearer of kin unto my mother than he is; neither think I myself either that unworthy or that near my end that I need to make such a Davidical testament,[35]

---

[31] inconveniences

[32] Because of his hope of being the next English monarch, James was extremely eager to remain in the good graces of England and Elizabeth. For examples of the kinds of diplomatic care his relations with England demanded of him (most acutely at the time of his mother's execution), see G. P. V. Akrigg, ed., *Letters of King James VI & I*, 57–207.

[33] reveal

[34] It is not clear what incident or saying James is referring to.

[35] David, on the point of death in old age, entreated his son Solomon to take

since I have ever thought it the duty of a worthy prince rather with a pike than a pen to write his just revenge. But in this matter I have no delight to be large, wishing all men to judge of my future projects according to my by-past actions.

Thus having as much insisted in the clearing of these two points as will, I hope, give sufficient satisfaction to all honest men, and leaving the envious to the food of their own venom, I will heartily pray thee, loving reader, charitably to conceive of my honest intention in this book. I know the greatest part of the people of this whole isle have been very curious for a sight thereof: some for the love they bear me, either being particularly acquainted with me or by a good report that perhaps they have heard of me, and therefore longed to see anything that proceeded from that author whom they so loved and honoured, since books are vive[36] ideas of the author's mind. Some only for mere curiosity, that think it their honour to know all new things, were curious to glut their eyes therewith only that they might vaunt them to have seen it; and some, fraughted with causeless envy at the author, did greedily search out the book, thinking their stomach fit enough for turning never so wholesome food into noisome and infective humours. So as this, their great concurrence in curiosity (though proceeding from far different complexions) hath enforced the untimous[37] divulgating[38] of this book far contrary to my intention, as I have already said. To which Hydra[39] of diversely inclined spectators I have no targe[40] to oppone[41] but plainness, patience, and sincerity: plainness for resolving and satisfying of the first sort; patience for to bear with the shallowness of the next; and sincerity to defy the malice of the third withal. Though I cannot please all men therein, I am contented so that I only please the virtuous sort; and though they also find not everything therein so fully to answer their expectation as the argument would seem to require, although I would wish them modestly to remember that God [has][42] not bestowed all his gifts upon one, but parted them by a

---

revenge on Joab, whom David resented for a number of offences (1 Kings 2:5–6).
[36] life-like
[37] unseasonable, premature
[38] publishing
[39] multi-headed monster in Greek mythology
[40] small shield
[41] oppose
[42] "hes" in original

justice distributive; and that many eyes see more than one; and that the variety of men's minds is such that "*tot capita tot sensus*";[43] yea, and that even the very faces that God hath by nature brought forth in the world do, every one in some of their particular lineaments, differ from any other. Yet in truth it was not my intention in handling of this purpose (as it is easy to perceive) fully to set down here all such grounds as might out of the best writers have been alleged and out of my own invention and experience added for the perfect institution of a king, but only to give some such precepts to my own son for the government of this kingdom as was meetest for him to be instructed in and best became me to be the informer of.

If I in this book have been too particularly plain, impute it to the necessity of the subject: not so much being ordained for the institution of a prince in general, as I have said, as containing particular precepts to my son in special, whereof he could have made but a general use if they had not contained the particular diseases of this kingdom, with the best remedies for the same, which it became me best as a king, having learned both the theoric and the practic[44] thereof, more plainly to express than any simple schoolman that only knows matters of kingdoms by contemplation.

But if in some places it seem too obscure, impute it to the shortness thereof, being both for the respect of myself and of my son constrained thereunto: my own respect for fault of leisure, being so continually occupied in the affairs of my office, as my great burden and restless fashery[45] is more than known to all that knows or hears of me; for my son's respect, because I know by myself that a prince, so long as he is young, will be so carried away with some sort of delight or other that he cannot patiently abide the reading of any large volume, and when he comes to a full maturity of age, he must be so busied in the active part of his charge as he will not be permitted to bestow many hours upon the contemplative part thereof: so as it was neither fit for him nor possible for me to have made this treatise any more ample than it is. Indeed I am little beholden to the curiosity of some who, thinking it too large already (as appears), for lack of leisure to copy it drew some notes out of it for speed's sake, putting

---

[43] so many heads, therefore so many viewpoints (slightly inaccurate quotation from Terence, *Phormio* 3.454).

[44] theory and practice

[45] worry

in the one half of the purpose and leaving out the other: not unlike the man that alleged that part of the Psalm, "*non est Deus*," but left out the preceeding words, "*Dixit insipiens in corde suo.*"[46] And of these notes, making a little pamphlet (lacking both my method and half of my matter), entitled it, forsooth,[47] *The King's Testament,* as if I had eked[48] a third testament of my own to the two that are in the Holy Scriptures. It is true that in a place thereof, for affirmation of the purpose I am speaking of to my son, I bring myself in there as speaking upon my testament; for in that sense every record in writ[49] of a man's opinion in anything (in respect that papers outlive their authors) is, as it were, a testament of that man's will in that case; and in that sense it is that in that place I call this treatise a testament. But from any particular sentence in a book to give the book itself a title is as ridiculous as to style the book of the Psalms the book of *Dixit Insipiens,* because with these words one of them doth begin.

Well, leaving these new baptizers and blockers[50] of other men's books to their own follies, I return to my purpose, anent the shortness of this book, suspecting that all my excuses for the shortness thereof shall not satisfy some, especially in our neighbour country, who thought that, as I have so narrowly in this treatise touched all the principal sicknesses in our kingdom with overtures for the remedies thereof, as I said before, so looked they to have found something therein that should have touched the sicknesses of their state in the like sort. But they will easily excuse me thereof if they will consider the form I have used in this treatise, wherein I only teach my son out of my own experience what form of government is fittest for this kingdom; and in one part thereof, speaking of the borders, I plainly there do excuse myself that I will speak nothing of the state of England, as a matter wherein I never had experience. I know, indeed, no kingdom lacks her own diseases, and likewise what interest I have in the prosperity of that state; for although I would be silent, my blood and descent [do][51] sufficiently proclaim it. But notwithstanding, since there is a lawful queen there presently reigning, who hath

---

[46]"The fool hath said in his heart, 'There is no God'" (Psalm 14:1).

[47]truly

[48]added

[49]a written work

[50]one who embosses the cover with the title (in bookbinding)

[51]"doth" in original

so long with so great wisdom and felicity governed her kingdoms as (I must in true sincerity confess) the like hath not been read nor heard of either in our time or since the days of the Roman emperor Augustus,[52] it could no ways become me, far inferior to her in knowledge and experience, to be a busybody in other princes' matters and to fish in other folks' waters, as the proverb is. No, I hope by the contrary (with God's grace) ever to keep that Christian rule, to do as I would be done to; and I doubt nothing, yea, even in her name I dare promise, by the by-past experience of her happy government, as I have already said, that no good subject shall be more careful to inform her of any corruptions stolen in her state than she shall be zealous, for the discharge of her conscience and honour, to see the same purged and restored to the ancient integrity; and further during her time becomes me least of any to meddle in.

And thus having resolved all the doubts, so far as I can imagine, may be moved against this treatise, it only rests to pray thee, charitable reader, to interpret favourably this birth of mine, according to the integrity of the author and not looking for perfection in the work itself. As for my part, I only glory thereof in this point: that I trust no sort of virtue is condemned nor any degree of vice allowed in it; and that, though it be not perhaps so gorgeously decked and richly attired as it ought to be, it is at the least rightly proportioned in all the members, without any monstrous deformity in any of them; and specially that, since it was first written in secret and is now published not of ambition but of a kind of necessity, it must be taken of all men for the true image of my very mind and form of the rule which I have prescribed to myself and mine, which as in all my actions I have hitherto pressed to express so far as the nature of my charge and the condition of time would permit me: so beareth it a discovery of that which may be looked for at my hand and whereto even in my secret thoughts I have engaged myself for the time to come. And thus in a firm trust that it shall please God, who with my being and crown gave me this mind to maintain and augment the same in me and my posterity, to the discharge of our conscience, the maintenance of our honour, and weal of our people, I bid thee heartily farewell.

---

[52] Augustus (63BCE–14CE), adopted son of Julius Caesar, was the first Roman emperor (23BCE–14CE). He was known for being an astute and effective administrator.

Prince Henry. Engraving by Cornelis Boel (c. 1612).
Reproduced by courtesy of Robert Spencer.

Of a King's Christian Duty Towards God

The First Book

As he cannot be thought worthy to rule and command others that cannot rule and daunton[1] his own proper affections and unreasonable appetites, so can he not be thought worthy to govern a Christian people, knowing and fearing God, that in his own person and heart feareth not and loveth not the divine Majesty. Neither can anything in his government succeed well with him (devise and labour as he list[2]), as coming from a filthy spring, if his person be unsanctified; for as that royal prophet saith, "Except the Lord build the house, they labour in vain that build it; except the Lord keep the city, the keepers watch it in vain,"[3] in respect the blessing of God hath only power to give the success thereunto; and as Paul saith, he "planteth, Apollo watereth, but it is God only that giveth the increase."[4] Therefore, my son, first of all things learn to know and love that God whom to ye have a double obligation: first, for that he made you a man; and next, for that he made you a little god to sit on his throne and rule over other men. Remember that, as in dignity he hath erected you above others, so ought ye in thankfulness towards him go as far beyond all others. A mote in another's eye is a beam into yours; a blemish in another is a leprous bile into you; and a venial sin[5] (as the Papists call it) in another is a great crime into you. Think not, therefore, that the highness of your dignity diminisheth your faults (much less

---

[1] subdue
[2] wishes
[3] Psalm 127:1
[4] 1 Corinthians 3:6
[5] a lesser, as opposed to a mortal or damnable, sin

giveth you a license to sin), but by the contrary your fault shall be aggravated according to the height of your dignity, any sin that ye commit not being a single sin, procuring but the fall of one, but being an exemplar sin, and therefore drawing with it the whole multitude to be guilty of the same. Remember, then, that this glistering worldly glory of kings is given them by God to teach them to press[6] so to glister and shine before their people in all works of sanctification and righteousness, that their persons as bright lamps of godliness and virtue may, going in and out before their people, give light to all their steps. Remember also that by the right knowledge and fear of God (which is the beginning of wisdom, as Solomon saith[7]) ye shall know all the things necessary for the discharge of your duty both as a Christian and as a king, seeing in him, as in a mirror, the course of all earthly things, whereof he is the spring and only mover.

Now the only way to bring you to this knowledge is diligently to read his word and earnestly to pray for the right understanding thereof. "Search the scriptures," saith Christ, "for they bear testimony of me,"[8] and "The whole scripture," saith Paul, "is given by inspiration of God and is profitable to teach, to convince, to correct, and to instruct in righteousness, that the man of God may be absolute, being made perfect unto all good works."[9] And most properly of any other belongeth the reading thereof unto kings, since, in that part of Scripture where the godly kings are first made mention of that were ordained to rule over the people of God,[10] there is an express and most notable exhortation and commandment given them to read and meditate in the law of God.[11] I join to this the careful hearing of the doctrine with attendance and reverence; for "Faith cometh by hearing," saith the same apostle.[12] But above all, beware ye wrest not the word to your own appetite, as over many do, making it like a bell to sound as ye please to interpret; but by the contrary, frame all your affections to follow precisely the rule there set down.

---

[6]strive
[7]Proverbs 9:10
[8]John 5:39
[9]2 Timothy 3:16–17
[10]For James's reading of the origins of kingship in Samuel, see *The True Law*.
[11]Deuteronomy 17:19
[12]Romans 10:17

The whole of Scripture chiefly containeth two things: a command and a prohibition, to do such things and to abstain from the contrary. Obey in both: neither think it enough to abstain from evil and do no good; nor think not that, if ye do many good things, it may serve you for a cloak to mix evil turns therewith. And as in these two points the whole Scripture principally consisteth, so in two degrees standeth the whole service of God by man: interior or upward, exterior or downward; the first by prayer in faith towards God, the next by works flowing therefrom before the world: which is nothing else but the exercise of religion towards God and of equity towards your neighbour.

As for the particular points of religion, I need not to dilate[13] them; I am no hypocrite: follow my footsteps and your own present education therein. I thank God I was never ashamed to give account of my profession, howsoever the malicious lying tongues of some have traduced me; and if my conscience had not resolved me that all my religion presently professed by me and my kingdom was grounded upon the plain words of the Scripture, without the which all points of religion are superfluous, as anything contrary to the same is abomination, I had never outwardly avowed it for pleasure or awe of any flesh.[14]

And as for the points of equity towards your neighbour, because that will fall in properly upon the second part, concerning a king's office, I leave it to the own room.[15]

For the first part, then, of man's service to his God, which is religion, that is the worship of God according to his revealed will: it is wholly grounded upon the Scripture, as I have already said, quickened by faith, and conserved by conscience. For the Scripture, I have now spoken of it in general; but that ye may the more readily make choice of any part thereof for your instruction or comfort, remember shortly this method.

The whole Scripture is dited[16] by God's spirit, thereby as by his lively word, to instruct and rule the whole church militant to the end

---

[13] relate, enlarge upon

[14] anybody

[15] "I leave it to the own room" would seem to mean "I leave it to its own room or place," meaning that James will discuss the king's duty to his neighbours in the second book of *Basilikon Doron*, which addresses the "king's office."

[16] composed

of the world. It is composed of two parts: the Old and New Testament. The ground of the former is the law, which showeth our sin and containeth justice; the ground of the other is Christ, who, pardoning sin, containeth grace. The sum of the law is the ten commandments, more largely dilated[17] in the books of Moses, interpreted and applied by the prophets; and by the histories are the examples showed of obedience or disobedience thereto and what *praemium* or *poena*[18] was accordingly given by God. But because no man was able to keep the law nor any part thereof, it pleased God of his infinite wisdom and goodness to incarnate his only Son in our nature for satisfaction of his justice in his suffering for us, that since we could not be saved by doing, we might at least be saved by believing.

The ground, therefore, of the word of grace is contained in the four histories of the birth, life, death, resurrection, and ascension of Christ. The larger interpretation and use thereof is contained in the Epistles of the apostles; and the practice in the faithful or unfaithful, with the history of the infancy and first progress of the church, is contained in their Acts.

Would ye, then, know your sin by the law? Read the books of Moses containing it. Would ye have a commentary thereupon? Read the prophets and likewise the books of the Proverbs and Ecclesiastes, written by that great pattern of wisdom, Solomon, which will not only serve you for instruction how to walk in the obedience of the law of God but is also so full of golden sentences and moral precepts in all things that can concern your conversation in the world as among all the profane philosophers and poets ye shall not find so rich a storehouse of precepts of natural wisdom agreeing with the will and divine wisdom of God. Would ye see how good men are rewarded and wicked punished? Look the historical parts of these same books of Moses, together with the histories of Joshua, the Judges, Ezra, Nehemiah, Esther, and Job, but especially the books of the Kings and Chronicles, wherewith ye ought to be familiarly acquainted; for there shall ye see yourself as in a mirror, in the catalogue either of the good or the evil kings.

Would ye know the doctrine, life, and death of our Saviour, Christ? Read the evangelists. Would ye be more particularly trained up in his

---

[17] "delated" in original; reported
[18] reward or punishment

school? Meditate upon the Epistles of the apostles. And would ye be acquainted with the practices of that doctrine in the persons of the primitive church? Cast up the apostles' Acts. And as to the apocryph[al] books,[19] I omit them because I am no Papist, as I said before, and indeed some of them are no ways like the ditement[20] of the spirit of God.

But when ye read the Scripture, read it with a sanctified and chaste heart; admire reverently such obscure places as ye understand not, blaming only your own capacity; read with delight the plain places and study carefully to understand those that are somewhat difficile;[21] press to be a good textuary,[22] for the Scripture is ever the best interpreter of itself; but press not curiously to seek out farther than is contained therein, for that were over unmannerly a presumption, to strive to be further upon God's secrets than he hath will ye be; for what he thought needful for us to know, that hath he revealed there. And delight most in reading such parts of the Scripture as may best serve for your instruction in your calling, rejecting foolish curiosities upon genealogies and contentions, "which are but vain and profit not," as Paul saith.[23]

Now as to faith, which is the nourisher and quickener of religion, as I have already said: it is a sure persuasion and apprehension of the promises of God, applying them to your soul; and therefore may it justly be called the golden chain that linketh the faithful soul to Christ. And because it groweth not in our garden but "is the free gift

---

[19] The Apocrypha are certain books of the early Greek Bible covering the period between the Old and New Testaments and not forming part of Hebrew Scripture. Traditionally accepted—with some sense of their questionable status—by the Christian Church, they were not accepted as Scripture by Reformation theologians such as Martin Luther. The Catholic Church reconfirmed their canonical status at the Council of Trent in 1548. In Britain, they were rejected or held in suspicion by most reformers, especially those in Scotland. They were, however, included in the Authorized King James Bible of 1611. After 1646 they became more and more marginalized in the Anglican Church.

[20] composition

[21] difficult

[22] a textual, especially biblical, scholar; one who adheres closely to the letter of Scripture

[23] Titus 3:9

of God," as the same apostle saith,[24] it must be nourished by prayer, which is nothing else but a friendly talking with God.

As for teaching you the form of your prayers, the Psalms of David are the meetest schoolmaster that ye can be acquainted with (next the prayer of our Saviour, which is the only rule of prayer), whereout of, as of most rich and pure fountains, ye may learn all form of prayer necessary for your comfort at all occasions. And so much the fitter are they for you than for the common sort, in respect the composer thereof was a king, and therefore best behoved to know a king's wants and what things were meetest to be required by a king at God's hand for remedy thereof.

Use often to pray when ye are quietest, especially forget it not in your bed how oft soever ye do it at other times; for public prayer serveth as much for example as for any particular comfort to the supplicant.

In your prayer be neither over-strange with God, like the ignorant, common sort that prayeth nothing but out of books, nor yet over-homely[25] with him, like some of the vain, pharisaical[26] Puritans, that think they rule him upon their fingers. The former way will breed an uncouth coldness in you towards him; the other will breed in you a contempt of him. But in your prayer to God speak with all reverence; for if a subject will not speak but reverently to a king, much less should any flesh presume to talk with God as with his companion.

Crave in your prayer not only things spiritual but also things temporal, sometimes of greater and sometimes of less consequence, that ye may lay up in store his grant of these things for confirmation of your faith and to be an arles-penny[27] unto you of his love. Pray as ye find your heart moveth you, *pro re nata*;[28] but see that ye suit[29] no unlawful things, as revenge, lust, or suchlike, for that prayer cannot

---

[24]Romans 5:15

[25]overly familiar

[26]The Pharisees were an austere Jewish religious party who opposed state and official religious authority; in the New Testament they oppose the teachings and practices of Christ. In James's time the word "Pharisee" was virtually synonymous with "hypocrite."

[27]money given in confirmation of a bargain

[28]as matters stand

[29]sue for

come of faith, "and whatsoever is done without faith is sin," as the apostle saith.[30]

When ye obtain your prayer, thank him joyfully therefor;[31] if otherwise, bear patiently, pressing to win him with importunity, as the widow did the unrighteous judge;[32] and if, notwithstanding thereof, ye be not heard, assure yourself God foreseeth that which ye ask is not for your weal; and learn in time so to interpret all the adversities that God shall send unto you; so shall ye in the middest of them not only be armed with patience but joyfully lift up your eyes from the present trouble to the happy end that God will turn it to. And when ye find it once so fall out by proof, arm yourself with the experience thereof against the next trouble, assuring yourself, though ye cannot in time of the shower see through the cloud, yet in the end shall ye find God sent it for your weal, as ye found in the former.

And as for conscience, which I called the conserver of religion, it is nothing else but the light of knowledge that God hath planted in man, which, ever watching over all his actions, as it beareth him a joyful testimony when he does right, so choppeth[33] it him with a feeling that he hath done wrong whenever he commiteth any sin. And surely, although this conscience be a great torture to the wicked, yet is it a great comfort to the godly, if we will consider it rightly. For have we not a great advantage that have within ourselves while we live here a count-book[34] and inventory of all the crimes that we shall be accused of, either at the hour of our death or at the great day of judgement, which, when we please (yea, though we forget) will chop and remember us to look upon it, that, while we have leisure and are here, we may remember to amend and so at the day of our trial compear[35] with "new and white garments washed in the blood of the lamb," as Saint John saith?[36] Above all then, my son, labour to keep

---

[30] Romans 14:23

[31] for that

[32] There are several references in the Bible to unjust treatment of widows: see, for example, Isaiah 10:2 and Malachi 3:5; there are, however, no references to pressing with importunity.

[33] strikes

[34] account book

[35] appear

[36] Revelation 7:14

sound this conscience, which many prattle of but over few feel; especially be careful to keep it free from two diseases wherewith it useth oft to be infected: to wit, leprosy and superstition; the former is the mother of atheism, the other of heresies. By a leprous conscience I mean "a cauterized conscience," as Paul calleth it,[37] being become senseless of sin through sleeping in a careless security, as King David's was after his murder and adultery ever till he was wakened by the prophet Nathan's similitude.[38] And by superstition I mean when one restrains himself to any other rule in the service of God than is warranted by the word, the only true square[39] of God's service.

As for a preservative against this leprosy, remember ever once in the four and twenty hours, either in the night or when ye are at greatest quiet, to call yourself to account of all your last day's actions, either wherein ye have committed things ye should not or omitted the things ye should do either in your Christian or kingly calling; and in that account, let not yourself be smoothed over with that flattering *philautia*,[40] which is overkindly a sickness to all mankind, but censure yourself as sharply as if ye were your own enemy, "For if ye judge yourself, ye shall not be judged," as the apostle saith;[41] and then according to your censure, reform your actions as far as ye may, eschewing ever willfully and wittingly to contrare[42] your conscience. For a small sin willfully committed, with a deliberate resolution to break the bridle of conscience therein, is far more grievous before God than a greater sin committed in a sudden passion, when conscience is asleep. Remember, therefore, in all your actions of the great account that ye are one day to make; in all the days of your life

---

[37] 1 Timothy 4:2

[38] The story of David's adultery with Bathsheba and his arrangement for the death of her husband, Uriah, is told in 2 Samuel 11; in 2 Samuel 12, the prophet Nathan procures David's repentance by recourse to the parable of a rich man who feeds a traveller with a poor man's single lamb rather than make use of his own great flocks.

[39] the instrument by which a carpenter measures the accuracy of his or her work; used here in the sense of guiding principle or measure

[40] self-love; in Greek letters in original

[41] 1 Corinthians 11:31

[42] oppose

ever learning to die and living every day as if it were your last, *"Omnem crede diem tibi diluxisse supremum."*[43]

And therefore I would not have you to pray with the Papists, to be preserved from sudden death, but that God would give you grace so to live as ye may every hour of your life be ready for death; so shall ye attain to the virtue of true fortitude, never being afraid for the horror of death, come when he list. And especially beware to offend your conscience with use of swearing or lying, suppose but in jest; for oaths are but an use[44] and a sin cloathed with no delight nor gain, and therefore the more inexcusable even in the sight of men; and lying cometh also much of a vile use, which banisheth shame. Therefore beware even to deny the truth, which is a sort of lie that may best be eschewed by a person of your rank. For if anything be asked at you that ye think not meet to reveal, if ye say that question is not pertinent for them to ask, who dare examine you further? And using sometimes this answer both in true and false things that shall be asked at you, such unmannerly people will never be the wiser thereof.

And for keeping your conscience sound from that sickness of superstition, ye must neither lay the safety of your conscience upon the credit of your own conceits nor yet of other men's humours, how great doctors of divinity that ever they be, but ye must only ground it upon the express Scripture; for conscience not grounded upon sure knowledge is either an ignorant fantasy or an arrogant vanity. Beware, therefore, in this case with two extremities: the one, to believe with the Papists the church's authority better than your own knowledge; the other, to lean with the Anabaptists to your own conceits and dreamed revelations.

But learn wisely to discern betwixt points of salvation and indifferent things, betwixt substance and ceremonies, and betwixt the express commandment and will of God in his word and the invention or ordinance of man, since all that is necessary for salvation is contained in the Scripture. For in anything that is expressly commanded or prohibited in the book of God, ye cannot be over-precise even in the least thing, counting every sin not according to the light estimation and common use of it in the world but as the book of God

---

[43] Believe every day that has dawned is the last for you (Horace, *Epistles* 1.4.13).

[44] habit

counteth of it. But as for all other things not contained in the Scripture, spare not to use or alter them as the necessity of the time shall require. And when any of the spiritual office-bearers in the church speak unto you anything that is well-warranted by the word, reverence and obey them as the heralds of the most high God; but if, passing that bounds, they urge you to embrace any of their fantasies in the place of God's word or would colour their particulars with a pretended zeal, acknowledge them for no other than vain men exceeding the bounds of their calling and, according to your office, gravely and with authority redact[45] them in order again.

To conclude, then, both this purpose of conscience and the first part of this book: keep God more sparingly in your mouth but abundantly in your heart; be precise in effect but social in show; kithe[46] more by your deeds than by your words the love of virtue and hatred of vice; and delight more to be godly and virtuous in deed than to be thought and called so, expecting more for your praise and reward in heaven than here; and apply to all your outward actions Christ's command to pray and give your alms secretly. So shall ye on the one part be inwardly garnished with true Christian humility, not outwardly (with the proud Pharisee) glorying in your godliness but saying, as Christ commandeth us all when we have done all that we can, "*Inutiles servi sumus.*"[47] And on the other part ye shall eschew outwardly before the world the suspicion of filthy, proud hypocrisy and deceitful dissimulation.

---

[45] to bring or reduce into a certain state
[46] make known
[47] We are unprofitable servants (Luke 17:10).

Of a King's Duty in His Office

The Second Book

But as ye are clothed with two callings, so must ye be alike careful for the discharge of them both, that as ye are a good Christian, so ye may be a good king, discharging your office (as I showed before) in the points of justice and equity, which in two sundry ways ye must do: the one in establishing and executing (which is the life of the law) good laws among your people; the other by your behaviour in your own person and with your servants, to teach your people by your example. For people are naturally inclined to counterfeit[1] (like apes) their prince's manners, according to the notable saying of Plato,[2] expressed by the poet:

> *Componitur orbis*
> *Regis ad exemplum; nec sic inflectere sensus*
> *Humanos edicta valent, quam vita regentis.*[3]

For the part of making and executing of laws, consider first the true difference betwixt a lawful, good king and an usurping tyrant, and ye shall the more easily understand your duty herein, for *contraria juxta se posita magis elucescunt.*[4] The one acknowledgeth himself ordained for his people, having received from God a burden of

---

[1]imitate

[2]Cicero attributes to Plato the assertion that the citizens of a commonwealth are usually like their leaders (*Epistulae ad Familiares* 1.9.12).

[3]The world is bound to the king's example; thus proclamations are not as important for influencing people's attitudes as the king's life is (Claudian, *Panegyricus de Quarto Consulatu Honorii Augusti* 299–301). Buchanan quotes this passage from Claudian in order to argue that kings, in order to set an example for the people, have a duty to obey the laws (84).

[4]Contraries placed beside each other become clearer.

113

government whereof he must be countable;[5] the other thinketh his
people ordained for him, a prey to his passions and inordinate appetites, as the fruits of his magnanimity.[6] And therefore, as their ends are
directly contrary, so are their whole actions as means whereby they
press to attain to their ends. A good king, thinking his highest honour
to consist in the due discharge of his calling, employeth all his study
and pains to procure and maintain, by the making and execution of
good laws, the welfare and peace of his people, and as their natural
father and kindly master, thinketh his greatest contentment standeth
in their prosperity and his greatest surety[7] in having their hearts,
subjecting his own private affections and appetites to the weal and
standing of his subjects, ever thinking the common interest his
chiefest particular; where, by the contrary, an usurping tyrant, thinking his greatest honour and felicity to consist in attaining, *per fas, vel
nefas,*[8] to his ambitious pretenses, thinketh never himself sure but by
the dissension and factions among his people, and counterfeiting the
saint while he once creep in credit, will then, by inverting all good
laws to serve only for his unruly private affections, frame the commonweal ever to advance his particular, building his surety upon his
people's misery, and in the end, as a stepfather and an uncouth
hireling, make up his own hand upon the ruins of the republic. And
according to their actions, so receive they their reward. For a good
king, after a happy and famous reign, dieth in peace, lamented by
his subjects and admired by his neighbours, and leaving a reverent
renown behind him in earth, obtaineth the crown of eternal felicity
in heaven. And although some of them (which falleth out very rarely)
may be cut off by the treason of some unnatural subjects, yet liveth
their fame after them, and some notable plague faileth never to
overtake the committers in this life, besides their infamy to all
posterities hereafter. Where, by the contrary, a tyrant's miserable and
infamous life armeth in end his own subjects to become his
burreaux,[9] and although that rebellion be ever unlawful on their part,
yet is the world so wearied of him that his fall is little meaned[10] by

---

[5]accountable
[6]magnificence
[7]security
[8]by divine will or wickedness
[9]executioners
[10]lamented

the rest of his subjects and but smiled at by his neighbours. And besides the infamous memory he leaveth behind him here and the endless pain he sustaineth hereafter, it oft falleth out that the committers not only escape unpunished but, farther, the fact will remain as allowed by the law in divers ages thereafter. It is easy then for you, my son, to make a choice of one of these two sorts of rulers by following the way of virtue to establish your standing; yea, in case ye fell in the highway, yet should it be with the honourable report and just regret of all honest men.

And therefore, to return to my purpose anent the government of your subjects by making and putting good laws to execution: I remit the making of them to your own discretion as ye shall find the necessity of new-rising corruptions to require them, for "*ex malis moribus bonae leges natae sunt*";[11] besides that in this country we have already more good laws than are well execute[d], and am only to insist in your form of government anent their execution. Only remember that, as Parliaments have been ordained for making of laws, so ye abuse not their institution in holding them for any men's particulars. For as a Parliament is the honourablest and highest judgement in the land (as being the king's head court) if it be well used, which is by making of good laws in it, so is it the injustest judgement seat that may be, being abused to men's particulars: irrevocable decreets[12] against particular parties being given therein under colour of general laws, and ofttimes the estates not knowing themselves whom thereby they hurt. And therefore hold no Parliaments but for necessity of new laws, which would be but seldom; for few laws and well put in execution are best in a well-ruled commonweal. As for the matter of forfeitures,[13] which also are done in Parliament, it is not good tigging[14] with these things; but my advice is ye forfeit none but for such odious crimes as may make them unworthy ever to be restored again. And for smaller offences, ye have other penalties sharp enough to be used against them.

And as for the execution of good laws, whereat I left, remember that, among the differences that I put betwixt the forms of the government

---

[11] Good laws are born of bad habits (Macrobius, *Saturnalia* 3.17.10).

[12] decrees

[13] "fore-faltures" in original; punishments or sanctions imposed on individuals by Parliament

[14] meddling

of a good king and an usurping tyrant, I show how a tyrant would enter like a saint while he found himself fast underfoot and then would suffer his unruly affections to burst forth. Therefore be ye contrare[15] at your first entry to your kingdom to that *Quinquennium Neronis*[16] with his tender-hearted wish, "*Vellem nescirem literas*,"[17] in giving the law full execution against all breakers thereof but[18] exception. For since ye come not to your reign *precario*,[19] nor by conquest, but by right and due descent, fear no uproars for doing of justice, since ye may assure yourself the most part of your people will ever naturally favour justice, providing always that ye do it only for love to justice and not for satisfying any particular passions of yours under colour thereof. Otherwise, how justly that ever the offender deserve it, ye are guilty of murder before God. For ye must consider that God ever looketh to your inward intention in all your actions.

And when ye have by the severity of justice once settled your countries and made them know that ye can strike, then may ye thereafter all the days of your life mix justice with mercy, punishing or sparing as ye shall find the crime to have been willfully or rashly committed and according to the by-past behaviour of the committer. For if otherwise ye kithe your clemency at the first, the offences would soon come to such heaps and the contempt of you grow so great that when ye would fall to punish, the number of them to be punished would exceed the innocent, and ye would be troubled to resolve whom at to begin and against your nature would be compelled then to wrack[20] many whom the chastisement of few in the beginning might have preserved. But in this my over-dear bought experience may serve you for a sufficient lesson. For I confess, where I thought by being gracious at the beginning to win all men's hearts to a loving and willing obedience, I by the contrary found the disorder of the country and the loss of my thanks to be all my reward.[21]

---

[15] contrary

[16] first five years of the reign of Nero

[17] I wish I didn't know how to write. This was Nero's response to a request to sign a death warrant (Seneca, *De Clementia* 2.1.2, and Suetonius, *Nero* 10.2).

[18] without

[19] upon request

[20] punish

[21] In *Measure for Measure,* a play written in conjunction with James's coming to the throne of England, Shakespeare deals with the very problem outlined by

But as this severe justice of yours upon all offences would be but for a time (as I have already said), so [are][22] there some horrible crimes that ye are bound in conscience never to forgive, such as witchcraft, willful murder, incest (especially within the degrees of consanguinity), sodomy,[23] poisoning, and false coin. As for offences against your own person and authority, since the fault concerneth yourself, I remit to your own choice to punish or pardon therein as

---

James. Duke Vincentio, discussing his own leniency, says:

> Now, as fond fathers,
> Having bound up the threat'ning twigs of birch,
> Only to stick it in their children's sight
> For terror, not to use, in time the rod
> Becomes more mock'd than fear'd; so our decrees,
> Dead to infliction, to themselves are dead,
> And liberty plucks justice by the nose;
> The baby beats the nurse, and quite athwart
> Goes all decorum. (I.iii.23–31)

Vincentio is afraid that after his long leniency, severity from him will appear "too dreadful" (34). He sets Angelo up to be severe on his behalf; however, Pompey points out that after the present excess of liberty, sexual restraint (which is the particular legal concern of the play) may only be achieved if the authorities "geld and splay all the youth of the city" (II.i.230-31). For extended discussions of the relations between *Basilikon Doron* and *Measure for Measure,* see David L. Stevenson, "The Role of James I in Shakespeare's *Measure for Measure,*" *ELH* 26 (1959): 188–208, and Terrell Tebbetts, "Talking Back to the King: *Measure for Measure* and the *Basilicon Doron,*" *College Literature* 12.2 (1985): 122–34. Note also Leeds Barroll's argument about the relations between Shakespeare and James in chapter two, "Shakespeare without King James," of *Politics, Plague, and Shakespeare's Theater: The Stuart Years.* Barroll argues, perhaps excessively, that "[t]he court and the king were not implicated in the dramatist's professional activities" (69). Further work remains to be done on the relations, literary, economic, and otherwise, between the Stuart court and Jacobean theater.

[22]"is" in original

[23]In the chapter on *Basilikon Doron* in his biography of James, David Mathew gives the following gloss:

> The word that makes me pause is sodomy. Little is known of the king's private life in 1599. It seems likely enough that he was then without a favourite. The king was fond of tumbling with his young men; perhaps he held that he did not complete the act which merited the severest penalties. (83)

your heart serveth you and according to the circumstances of the turn and the quality of the committer.

Here would I also eke another crime to be unpardonable, if I should not be thought partial, but the fatherly love I bear you will make me break the bounds of shame in opening it unto you. It is, then, the false and unreverent writing or speaking of malicious men against your parents and predecessors: ye know the command in God's law, "Honour your father and mother,"[24] and consequently, since ye are the lawful magistrate, suffer not both your princes and your parents to be dishonoured by any, especially since the example also toucheth yourself, in leaving thereby to your successors the measure of that which they shall meet out again to you in your like behalf. I grant we have all our faults, which privately betwixt you and God should serve you for examples to meditate upon and mend in your person, but should not be a matter of discourse to others whatsoever. And since ye are come of as honourable predecessors as any prince living, repress the insolence of such as, under pretence to tax a vice in the person, seek craftily to stain the race and to steal the affection of the people from their posterity. For how can they love you that hated them whom of ye are come? Wherefore destroy men innocent, young, sucking wolves and foxes but for the hatred they bear to their race? And why will a colt of a courser of Naples give a greater price in a market than an ass-colt but for love of the race? It is, therefore, a thing monstrous to see a man love the child and hate the parents, as on the other part the infaming[25] and making odious of the parent is the readiest way to bring the son in contempt. And for conclusion of this point, I may also allege my own experience. For besides the judgements of God that with my eyes I have seen fall upon all them that were chief traitors to my parents, I may justly affirm I never found yet a constant biding by me in all my straits by any that were of perfect age in my parents' days but only by such as constantly bode by them; I mean specially by them that served the queen my mother; for so that I discharge my conscience to you, my son, in revealing to you the truth, I care not what any traitor or treason-allower think of it.[26]

---

[24] Exodus 20:12

[25] defaming

[26] It is difficult to surmise to whom James is referring here. The civil war and regency period was not known for strong loyalty, and none of the principal figures who supported Mary later showed particularly noteworthy support of James.

And although the crime of oppression[27] be not in this rank of unpardonable crimes, yet the over-common use of it in this nation, as if it were a virtue, especially by the greatest rank of subjects in the land, requireth the king to be a sharp censurer thereof. Be diligent, therefore, to try and awful to beat down the horns of proud oppressors; embrace the quarrel of the poor and distressed as your own particular, thinking it your greatest honour to oppress the oppressors; care for the pleasure of none, neither spare ye any pains in your own person, to see their wrongs redressed; and remember of the honourable style given to my grandfather of worthy memory in being called "the poor man's king."[28] And as the most part of a king's office standeth in deciding that question of *meum* and *tuum*[29] among his subjects, so remember when ye sit in judgement that the throne ye sit on is God's, as Moses saith, and sway neither to the right hand nor to the left,[30] either loving the rich or pitying the poor. Justice should be blind and friendless; it is not there ye should reward your friends or seek to cross your enemies.

Here now, speaking of oppressors and of justice, the purpose leadeth me to speak of highland and border oppressions. As for the highlands, I shortly comprehend them all in two sorts of people: the one that dwelleth in our main land, that are barbarous for the most part and yet mixed with some show of civility; the other that dwelleth in the isles and are all-utterly[31] barbars[32] without any sort or show of civility. For the first sort, put straightly to execution the laws made already by me against their overlords and the chiefs of their clans, and it will be no difficulty to daunton them. As for the other sort, follow forth the course that I have intended in planting colonies among them of answerable inlands subjects, that within short time

---

[27] wrongful exercise of authority; unjust treatment of inferiors

[28] See, for example, John Knox's 1584 *History of the Reformation in Scotland* (ed. William Croft Dickinson [London: Thomas Nelson, 1949]):

> He was called of some a good poor man's King: of others he was
> termed a murderer of the nobility, and one that had decreed their
> whole destruction. Some praised him for the repressing of theft
> and oppression; others dispraised him for the defouling of men's
> wives and virgins. (1.40–41)

[29] mine and yours

[30] Deuteronomy 1:17, 17:20

[31] completely, absolutely

[32] barbarians

may reform and civilize the best inclined among them, rooting out or transporting the barbarous and stubborn sort and planting civility in their rooms.

But as for the borders, because I know, if ye enjoy not this whole isle according to God's right and your lineal descent, ye will never get leave to brook[33] this north and barrenest part thereof, no, not your own head whereon the crown should stand, I need not in that case trouble you with them; for then they will be the middest of the isle, and so as easily ruled as any part thereof.

And that ye may the readier with wisdom and justice govern your subjects by knowing what vices they are naturally most inclined to, as a good physician who must first know what peccant[34] humours his patient naturally is most subject unto before he can begin his cure, I shall therefore shortly note unto you the principal faults that every rank of the people of this country is most affected unto. And as for England, I will not speak begess[35] of them, never having been among them, although I hope in that God who ever favoureth the right before I die to be as well acquainted with their fashions.

As the whole subjects of our country by the ancient and fundamental policy of our kingdom are divided into three estates,[36] so is every estate hereof generally subject to some special vices, which in a manner by long habitude are thought rather virtue than vice among them; not that every particular man in any of these ranks of men is subject unto them, for there is good and evil of all sorts, but that I mean I have found by experience these vices to have taken greatest hold with these ranks of men.

And first, that I prejudge[37] not the church of her ancient privileges, reason would she should have the first place for order's sake in this catalogue.

The natural sickness that hath ever troubled and been the decay of all the churches since the beginning of the world, changing the candlestick from one to another, as John saith,[38] hath been pride,

---

[33] enjoy, possess

[34] sinning, offending

[35] by guess

[36] James here discusses each of the three estates: the church, the nobility, and the bourgeoisie.

[37] to affect prejudicially or injuriously

[38] Revelation 2:5

ambition, and avarice; and now last these same infirmities wrought the overthrow of the popish church in this country and divers others. But the reformation of religion in Scotland being extraordinarily wrought by God, wherein many things were inordinately done by a popular tumult and rebellion of such as blindly were doing the work of God but clogged with their own passions and particular respects, as well appeared by the destruction of our policy, and not proceeding from the prince's order as it did in our neighbour country of England, as likewise in Denmark and sundry parts of Germany,[39] some fiery spirited men in the ministry got such a guiding of the people at that time of confusion as, finding the gust[40] of government sweet, they begouth[41] to fantasy to themselves a democratic form of government, and having by the iniquity of time been over-well baited upon the wrack first of my grandmother and next of mine own mother,[42] and after usurping the liberty of the time in my long minority, settled themselves so fast upon[43] that imagined democracy, as they fed themselves with the hope to become *tribuni plebis*,[44] and so in a popular government by leading the people by the nose to bear the sway of all the rule. And for this cause there never rose faction in the time of my minority, nor trouble sensyne,[45] but they

---

[39] In England the reformation had come about as state policy of Henry VIII; in Denmark Christian III (1503–1559), a Lutheran, had overcome Catholic resistance in a civil war (1534–1536); in northern Germany the Schmalkadic League, led by Prince Philip of Hesse (1504–1567), had been founded in 1531 to resist the Catholic emperor Charles V. In James's view, the reformation in Scotland had been the work of men like John Knox and Andrew Melville who had, more often than not, fostered resistance to royal authority and undermined state policy.

[40] taste

[41] began

[42] Mary of Guise, after the death of James V, and Mary Queen of Scots, both Catholic sympathizers, were involved in disastrous struggles with John Knox and other reformers.

[43] became so firmly attached to

[44] tribunes of the people: representatives of the populace in the Roman republic. Marginal note: "Such were the Demagogi at Athens." The demagogues—"leaders of the people"—were political figures in Athens in the latter part of the fifth century BCE. They were known for their rhetorical and administrative skill and were commonly depicted as self-serving, manipulative, and crass.

[45] since then

that were upon that factious part were ever careful to persuade and allure these unruly spirits among the ministry to spouse[46] that quarrel as their own, wherethrough I was ofttimes calumniated in their popular sermons, not for any evil or vice in me but because I was a king, which they thought the highest evil.[47] And because they were ashamed to profess this quarrel, they were busy to look narrowly in all my actions; and I warrant you a mote in my eye, yea, a false report, was matter enough for them to work upon; and yet for all their cunning, whereby they pretended to distinguish the lawfulness of the office from the vice of the person, some of them would sometimes snapper[48] out well-grossly with the truth of their intentions, informing the people that all kings and princes were naturally enemies to the liberty of the church and could never patiently bear the yoke of Christ: with such sound doctrine fed they their flocks. And because the learned, grave, and honest men of the ministry were ever ashamed and offended with their temerity and presumption, pressing by all good means by their authority and example to reduce them to a greater moderation, there could be no way found out so meet in their conceit that were turbulent spirits among them for maintaining their plots, as parity[49] in the church, whereby the ignorants were emboldened as bards[50] to cry the learned, godly, and modest out of it: parity, the mother of confusion and enemy to unity, which is the mother of order. For if, by the example thereof once established in the ecclesiastical government, the politic and civil estate should be drawn to the like, the great confusion that thereupon would arise may easily be discerned. Take heed, therefore, my son, to such Puritans, very pests in the church and commonweal, whom no deserts can oblige, neither oaths or promises bind, breathing nothing but sedition and calumnies, aspiring without measure, railing without reason, and making their own imaginations (without any warrant of the Word) the square of their conscience. I protest before the great God, and since I am here as upon my testament, it is no place for me

---

[46] espouse

[47] The most famous example of such activity was a sermon delivered in 1596 by David Black, minister of Saint Andrew's, in which all kings were associated with the devil and Queen Elizabeth was called an atheist.

[48] trip or stumble

[49] equality and lack of hierarchy among ministers in the church

[50] strolling musicians (a term of contempt)

to lie in, that ye shall never find with any highland or border thieves greater ingratitude and more lies and vile perjuries than with these fanatic spirits. And suffer not the principals of them to brook your land, if ye like to sit at rest, except ye would keep them for trying your patience, as Socrates did an evil wife.[51]

And for preservative against their poison, entertain and advance the godly, learned, and modest men of the ministry, whom of (God be praised) there lacketh not a sufficient number; and by their provision to bishoprics[52] and benefices,[53] annulling that vile Act of Annexation[54] if ye find it not done to your hand, ye shall not only banish their conceited parity, whereof I have spoken, and their other imaginary grounds, which can neither stand with the order of the church nor the peace of a commonweal and well-ruled monarchy, but ye shall also re-establish the old institution of three estates in Parliament, which can no otherwise be done.[55] But in this I hope, if God spare me days, to make you a fair entry; always where I leave, follow ye my steps.

And to end my advice anent the church estate, cherish no man more than a good pastor, hate no man more than a proud Puritan: thinking it one of your fairest styles to be called a loving nourish-father to the church; seeing all the churches within your dominions planted with good pastors, the schools (the seminary of the church) maintained, the doctrine and discipline preserved in purity according to God's word, a sufficient provision for their sustentation, a comely order in their policy, pride punished, humility advanced, and they so to reverence their superiors, and their flocks them, as the flourishing of your church in piety, peace, and learning may be one of the

---

[51]The marginal note in the 1616 *Workes* reads "Xantippe." In his *Symposium*, Xenophon writes that Socrates claimed he kept a difficult wife so that, by learning to get along with her, he could more easily bear with all other people (2.10).

[52]office of a bishop. The episcopacy had suffered greatly under the reforms of the kirk, and one aspect of James's ongoing struggle with the reformers had to do with his desire to restore bishops to their earlier place of prominence—he met, however, with very limited success.

[53]ecclesiastical position with income

[54]The Act of Annexation of 1587, by which the state confiscated church property, had, for James, the unfortunate effect of entrenching the reformers and undermining bishoprics and church hierarchy without providing any actual new wealth for the government.

[55]The church was traditionally represented by bishops in the House of Lords.

chief points of your earthly glory, being ever alike ware[56] with both the extremities; as well as ye repress the vain Puritan, so not to suffer proud papal bishops, but as some for their qualities will deserve to be preferred before others, so chain them with such bonds as may preserve that estate from creeping to corruption.

The next estate now that by order cometh in purpose, according to their ranks in Parliament, is the nobility, although second in rank yet over-far first in greatness and power either to do good or evil, as they are inclined.

The natural sickness that I have perceived this estate subject to in my time hath been a feckless,[57] arrogant conceit of their greatness and power, drinking in with their very nourish-milk that their honour stood in committing three points of iniquity: to thrall[58] by oppression the meaner sort that dwelleth near them to their service and following, although they hold nothing of them; to maintain their servants and dependers in any wrong, although they be not answerable to the laws (for anybody will maintain his man in a right cause); and for any displeasure that they apprehend to be done unto them by their neighbour, to take up a plain feid[59] against him and (without respect to God, king, or commonweal) to bang it out bravely, he and all his kin against him and all his; yea, they will think the king far in their common in case they agree to grant an assurance to a short day for keeping of the peace, where, by their natural duty, they are oblished[60] to obey the law and keep the peace all the days of their life, upon the peril of their very craigs.[61]

For remeid[62] to these evils in their estate, teach your nobility to keep your laws as precisely as the meanest; fear not their orping[63] or being discontented, as long as ye rule well; for their pretended reformation of princes taketh never effect but where evil government preceedeth. Acquaint yourself so with all the honest men of your barons and gentlemen, and be in your giving access so open and

---

[56] wary
[57] ineffective
[58] enslave
[59] feud
[60] obliged
[61] necks
[62] remedy
[63] fretting

affable to every rank of honest persons as may make them pert,[64] without scaring at[65] you to make their own suits to you themselves and not to employ the great lords their intercessors, for intercession to saints is papistry; so shall ye bring to a measure their monstrous backs.[66] And for their barbarous feids, put the laws to due execution made by me there-anent, beginning ever rathest[67] at him that ye love best and is most oblished unto you, to make him an example to the rest. For ye shall make all your reformations to begin at your elbow, and so by degrees to flow to the extremities of the land. And rest not until ye root out these barbarous feids, that their effects may be as well smoared[68] down as their barbarous name is unknown to any other nation. For if this treatise were written either in French or Latin, I could not get them named unto you but by circumlocution. And for your easier abolishing of them, put sharply to execution my laws made against guns and traitorous pistolets, thinking in your heart, terming in your speech, and using by your punishments all such as wear and use them as brigands and cutthroats.

On the other part, eschew the other extremity, in lightlying[69] and contemning your nobility. Remember how that error [broke][70] the king my grandfather's heart.[71] But consider that virtue followeth oftest noble blood; the worthiness of their antecessors craveth a reverent regard to be had unto them: honour them, therefore, that are obedient to the law among them as peers and fathers of your land; the more frequently that your court can be garnished with them, think it the more your honour, acquainting and employing them in all your greatest affairs, since it is they must be your arms and executors of your laws; and so use yourself lovingly to the obedient and rigourously to the stubborn, as may make the greatest of them to think that the chiefest point of their honour standeth in striving with the meanest of the land in humility towards you and obedience

---

[64]aware

[65]being afraid of

[66]forces

[67]"rathest" is the superlative form of "rather"

[68]choked

[69]disparaging

[70]"brake" in original

[71]James V ran into conflict with his barons, who leant him little support in the war with England that hastened his death in 1542.

to your laws, beating ever in their ears that one of the principal points of service that ye crave of them is in their persons to practice, and by their power to procure, due obedience to the law, without the which no service they can make can be agreeable unto you.

But the greatest hindrance to the execution of our laws in this country are these heritable sheriffdoms[72] and regalities,[73] which, being in the hands of the great men, do wrack the whole country. For which I know no present remedy but by taking the sharper account of them in their offices, using all punishment against the slothful that the law will permit; and ever as they vaik,[74] for any offences committed by them dispone[75] them never heritably again, pressing with time to draw it to the laudable custom of England, which ye may the easilier do being king of both, as I hope in God ye shall.

And as to the third and last estate, which is our burghs[76] (for the small barons are but an inferior part of the nobility and of their estate), they are composed of two sorts of men: merchants and craftsmen, either of these sorts being subject to their own infirmities.

The merchants think the whole commonweal ordained for making them up, and accounting it their lawful gain and trade to enrich themselves upon the loss of all the rest of the people, they transport from us things necessary, bringing back sometimes unnecessary things and at other times nothing at all. They buy for us the worst wares and sell them at the dearest prices; and albeit the victuals[77] fall or rise of their prices according to the abundance or scantness thereof, yet the prices of their wares ever rise but never fall, being as constant in that their evil custom as if it were a settled law for them. They are also the special cause of the corruption of the coin, transporting all our own and bringing in foreign upon what price they please to set on it. For order putting to them, put the good laws in execution that are already made anent these abuses; but especially do three things: establish honest, diligent, but few searchers,[78] for

---

[72] territory under the jurisdiction of a sheriff

[73] territorial jurisdiction of a royal nature granted by a king

[74] become vacant

[75] grant

[76] towns

[77] livestock and raw materials

[78] custom house officers appointed to search ships

many hands make slight work, and have an honest and diligent thesaurer[79] to take count of them; permit and allure foreign merchants to trade here, so shall ye have best and best cheap wares, not buying them at the third hand; and set every year down a certain price of all things, considering first how it is in other countries, and the price being set reasonably down, if the merchants will not bring them home on the price, cry foreigners free to bring them.

And because I have made mention here of the coin, make your money of fine gold and silver, causing the people be paid with substance and not abused with number; so shall ye enrich the commonweal and have a great treasure laid up in store if ye fall in wars or in any straits. For the making it baser will breed your commodity;[80] but it is not to be used but at a great necessity.

And the craftsmen think we should be content with their work how bad and dear soever it be; and if they in anything be controlled, up goeth the blue blanket.[81] But for their part, take example by England, how it hath flourished both in wealth and policy since the strangers' craftsmen came in among them. Therefore, not only permit but allure strangers to come here also, taking as strait[82] order for repressing the mutin[y]ing of ours at them as was done in England at their first in-bringing there.

But unto one fault is all the common people of this kingdom subject, as well burgh as land, which is to judge and speak rashly of their prince, setting the commonweal upon four props,[83] as we call it, ever wearying of the present estate and desirous of novelties. For remedy whereof (besides the execution of laws that are to be used against unreverent speakers) I know no better mean than so to rule as may justly stop their mouths from all such idle and unreverent speeches, and so to prop the weal of your people with provident care for their good government, that justly Momus himself may have no ground to grudge at; and yet so to temper and mix your severity with mildness that, as the unjust railers may be restrained with a reverent

---

[79] treasurer

[80] profit

[81] banner or standard of the Incorporated Trades Guild of Edinburgh

[82] strict

[83] The exact meaning of this phrase is obscure; the Latin translation of 1604, however, reads "*in lubrico & ancipiti loco*," or "in a slippery and uncertain situation."

awe, so the good and loving subjects may not only live in surety and wealth but be stirred up and invited by your benign courtesies to open their mouths in the just praise of your so well moderated regiment. In respect whereof, and therewith also the more to allure them to a common amity among themselves, certain days in the year would be appointed for delighting the people with public spectacles of all honest games and exercise of arms, as also for convening of neighbours, for entertaining friendship and heartliness by honest feasting and merriness. For I cannot see what greater superstition can be in making plays and lawful games in May and good cheer at Christmas than in eating fish in Lent and upon Fridays, the Papists as well using the one as the other, so that always the Sabbaths be kept holy and no unlawful pastime be used. And as this form of contenting the people's minds hath been used in all well-governed republics, so will it make you to perform in your government that old good sentence, "*Omne tulit punctum qui miscuit utile dulci.*"[84]

Ye see now, my son, how, for the zeal I bear to acquaint you with the plain and single verity of all things, I have not spared to be something satiric in touching well quickly the faults in all the estates of my kingdom. But I protest before God, I do it with the fatherly love that I owe to them all, only hating their vices, whereof there is a good number of honest men free in every estate.

And because for the better reformation of all these abuses among your estates it will be a great help unto you to be well-acquainted with the nature and humours of all your subjects and to know particularly the estate of every part of your dominions, I would therefore counsel you once in the year to visit the principal parts of the country ye shall be in for the time, and because I hope ye shall be king of more countries than this, once in the three years to visit all your kingdoms,[85] not lippening[86] to viceroys but hearing yourself their complaints, and having ordinary councils and justice seats in every kingdom of their own countrymen and the principal matters ever to be decided by yourself when ye come in those parts.

---

[84] He who has mixed usefulness and pleasure has carried every vote (Horace, *Ars Poetica* 343).

[85] In actual practice, after leaving Scotland for England in 1603, James returned to Scotland only once, in 1617.

[86] trusting

Ye have also to consider that ye must not only be careful to keep your subjects from receiving any wrong of others within, but also ye must be careful to keep them from the wrong of any foreign prince without, since the sword is given you by God not only to revenge upon your own subjects the wrongs committed amongst themselves but, further, to revenge and free them of foreign injuries done unto them. And therefore wars upon just quarrels are lawful; but, above all, let not the wrong cause be on your side.

Use all other princes as your brethren, honestly and kindly. Keep precisely your promise unto them, although to your hurt. Strive with every one of them in courtesy and thankfulness, and as with all men, so especially with them be plain and truthful, keeping ever that Christian rule "to do as ye would be done to," especially in counting rebellion against any other prince a crime against your own self, because of the preparative.[87] Supply not, therefore, nor trust not other princes' rebels, but pity and succour all lawful princes in their troubles. But if any of them will not abstain, notwithstanding whatsoever your good deserts, to wrong you or your subjects, crave redress at leisure; hear and do all reason; and if no offer that is lawful or honourable can make him to abstain nor repair his wrongdoing, then for last refuge commit the justness of your cause to God, giving first honestly up with him and in a public and honourable form.

But omitting now to teach you the form of making wars because that art is largely treated of by many[88] and is better learned by practice than speculation, I will only set down to you here a few precepts therein. Let first the justness of your cause be your greatest strength, and then omit not to use all lawful means for backing of the same. Consult, therefore, with no necromancer[89] nor false prophet upon

---

[87] that which prepares the way for something else

[88] In this regard, the marginal reference mentions Propertius, *Elegiae* 4; Lucan, *De Bello Civili;* Varro, *De Vita Populi Romani.*

[89] James discusses necromancy in his *Dæmonologie* (1597), especially book one, chapters two to four. In book one, chapter three of *Dæmonologie,* Philomathes asks Epistemon the following: "I would gladlie first heare, what thing it is that ye call *Magie* or *Necromancie."* Epistemon responds with the following: "This worde *Magie* in the *Persian* toung, importes as muche as to be ane contemplator or Interpretour of Divine and heavenlie sciences .... And this word *Necromancie* is a Greek word ... which is to say, the Prophecie by the dead. This last name is given, to this black & unlawfull science by the figure *Synecdoche,* because it is a principal part of that art, to serue them selues with

the success of your wars, remembering on King Saul's miserable end,[90] but keep your land clean of all soothsayers, according to the command in the law of God dilated[91] by Jeremiah.[92] Neither commit your quarrel to be tried by a duel; for beside that generally all duel appeareth to be unlawful, committing the quarrel, as it were, to a lot, whereof there is no warrant in the Scripture since the abrogating of the old law, it is specially most unlawful in the person of a king, who, being a public person, hath no power therefor[93] to dispose of himself, in respect that to his preservation or fall the safety or wrack of the whole commonweal is necessarily coupled, as the body is to the head.

Before ye take on war, play the wise king's part described by Christ,[94] foreseeing how ye may bear it out with all necessary provision; especially remember that money is "*nervus belli.*"[95] Choose old, experimented[96] captains and young, able soldiers. Be extremely strait and severe in martial discipline, as well for keeping of order, which is as requisite as hardiness in the wars, and punishing of sloth, which at a time may put the whole army in hazard, as likewise for repressing of mutinies, which in wars are wonderful dangerous. And look to the Spaniard, whose great success in all his wars hath only come through straitness of discipline and order; for such errors may be committed in the wars as cannot be gotten mended again.

Be in your own person wakerife,[97] diligent, and painful,[98] using the advice of such as are skilfullest in the craft, as ye must also do in all other. Be homely with your soldiers as your companions, for winning their hearts, and extremely liberal, for then is no time of sparing. Be cold and foreseeing in devising, constant in your resolutions, and forward and quick in your executions. Fortify well your

---

dead carcages [carcases] in their diuinations" (Craigie, *Minor Prose* 6).

[90]After the death of Samuel, Saul, in his fear of the Philistines, employed a witch to conjure up the ghost of Samuel. Samuel's ghost told Saul that God had deserted him and that David would be the new king (1 Samuel 28).

[91]set forth or reported on

[92]Jeremiah 27:9

[93]possibly therefore

[94]Luke 14:31

[95]the sinew or strength of war (Cicero, *Philippics* 5.2.5)

[96]experienced

[97]vigilant

[98]painstaking

camp and assail not rashly without an advantage; neither fear nor lightly your enemy. Be curious in devising strategems, but always honestly; for of anything they work greatest effects in the wars if secrecy be joined to invention. And once or twice in your own person hazard yourself fairly; but having acquired so the fame of courage and magnanimity, make not a daily soldier of yourself, exposing rashly your person to every peril; but conserve yourself thereafter for the weal of your people, for whose sake ye must more care for yourself than for your own.

And as I have counselled you to be slow in taking on a war, so advise I you to be slow in peacemaking. Before ye agree, look that the ground of your wars be satisfied in your peace and that ye see a good surety for you and your people; otherwise a[n] honourable and just war is more tolerable than a dishonourable and disadvantageous peace.

But it is not enough to a good king, by the scepter of good laws well-executed to govern, and by force of arms to protect his people, if he join not therewith his virtuous life in his own person and in the person of his court and company: by good example alluring his subjects to the love of virtue and hatred of vice. And therefore, my son, since all people are naturally inclined to follow their prince's example (as I showed you before), let it not be said that ye command others to keep the contrary course to that which in your own person ye practice, making so your words and deeds to fight together; but by the contrary, let your own life be a law book and a mirror to your people, that therein they may read the practice of their own laws and therein they may see by your image what life they should lead.

And this example in your own life and person I likewise divide in two parts: the first, in the government of your court and followers in all godliness and virtue; the next, in having your own mind decked and enriched so with all virtuous qualities that therewith ye may worthily rule your people. For it is not enough that ye have and retain (as prisoners) within yourself never so many good qualities and virtues except ye employ them and set them on work for the weal of them that are committed to your charge: "*Virtutis enim laus omnis in actione consistit.*"[99]

First, then, as to the government of your court and followers, King David sets down the best precepts that any wise and Christian king

---

[99] For the value of all virtue consists in action (Cicero, *De Officiis* 1.6.19).

can practice in that point.[100] For as ye ought to have a great care for the ruling well of all your subjects, so ought ye to have a double care for the ruling well of your own servants, since unto them ye are both a politic and economic[101] governor. And as every one of the people will delight to follow the example of any of the courtiers, as well in evil as in good, so what crime so horrible can there be committed and overseen in a courtier that will not be an exemplar excuse for any other boldly to commit the like? And therefore in two points have ye to take good heed anent your court and household: first, in choosing them wisely; next, in carefully ruling them whom ye have chosen.

It is an old and true saying that a kindly aver[102] will never become a good horse; for albeit good education and company be great helps to nature, and education be, therefore, most justly called *altera natura*,[103] yet it is evil[104] to get out of the flesh that is bred in the bone, as the old proverb saith. Be very ware, then, in making choice of your servants and company, "*Nam / Turpius ejicitur quam non admittitur hospes*,"[105] and many respects may lawfully let an admission that will not be sufficient causes of deprivation.

All your servants and court must be composed partly of minors, such as young lords, to be brought up in your company, or pages and suchlike, and partly of men of perfect age, for serving you in such rooms as ought to be filled with men of wisdom and discretion. For the first sort, ye can do no more but choose them within age that are come of a good and virtuous kind, *in fide parentum*,[106] as baptism is used. For though *anima non venit ex traduce*[107] but is immediately created by God and infused from above, yet it is most certain that virtue or vice will oftentimes with the heritage be transferred from the parents to the posterity and run on a blood, as the proverb is, the

---

[100] See Psalm 101

[101] household

[102] an old or worthless horse

[103] second nature

[104] difficult

[105] For it is more disgraceful for a guest to be driven out than not to be admitted (Ovid, *Tristia* 5.6.13).

[106] in the faith of the parents

[107] The soul does not come out of the vine. Traducianism was the belief that the soul was transmitted in procreation from parents to child.

sickness of the mind becoming as kindly[108] to some races as these sicknesses of the body that infect in the seed.[109] Especially choose such minors as are come of a true and honest race and have not had the house whereof they are descended infected with falsehood.

And as for the other sort of your company and servants that ought to be of perfect age: first, see that they be of a good fame and without blemish; otherwise what can the people think but that ye have chosen a company unto you according to your own humour and so have preferred these men for the love of their vices and crimes that ye knew them to be guilty of? For the people that see you not within cannot judge of you but according to the outward appearance of your actions and company, which only is subject to their sight. And next, see that they be endued[110] with such honest qualities as are meet for such offices as ye ordain them to serve in, that your judgement may be known in employing every man according to his gifts. And shortly, follow good King David's counsel in the choice of your servants, by setting your eyes upon the faithful and upright of the land to dwell with you.

But here I must not forget to remember and, according to my fatherly authority, to charge you to prefer specially to your service so many as have truly served me and are able for it, the rest, honourably to reward them, preferring their posterity before others, as kindliest.[111] So shall ye not only be best served (for if the haters of your parents cannot love you, as I showed before, it followeth of necessity their lovers must love you) but, further, ye shall kithe your thankful memory of your father and procure the blessing of these old servants in not missing their old master in you, which otherwise would be turned in a prayer for me and a curse for you. Use them, therefore, when God shall call me, as the testimonies of your affec-

---

[108] natural

[109] The marginal note in the 1616 *Workes* reads: "Witness the experience of the late house of Gowrie." James claimed that in August 1600 the Earl of Gowrie and his brother had lured him in bizarre circumstances to their house in Perth where they had made an attempt on his life. These brothers were the sons of the Earl of Gowrie, who had kidnapped James in 1582, and grandsons of the Earl of Ruthven, who had taken a leading role in the murder of Queen Mary's secretary David Riccio in 1566.

[110] endowed; "indued" in original

[111] (as is) most natural, most proper or fitting

tion towards me, trusting and advancing those farthest whom I found faithfullest, which ye must not discern by their rewards at my hand (for rewards, as they are called *bona fortunæ*,[112] so are they subject unto fortune) but according to the trust I gave them, having ofttimes had better heart than hap[113] to the rewarding of sundry. And on the other part, as I wish you to kithe your constant love towards them that I loved, so desire I you to kithe in the same measure your constant hatred to them that I hated. I mean, bring not home nor restore not such as ye find standing banished or forfeited[114] by me. The contrary would kithe in you over great a contempt of me and lightness in your own nature, for how can they be true to the son that were false to the father?

But to return to the purpose anent the choice of your servants, ye shall by this wise form of doing eschew the inconvenience that in my minority I fell in anent the choice of my servants. For by them that had the command where I was brought up were my servants put unto me, not choosing them that were meetest to serve me, but whom they thought meetest to serve their turn about me, as kithed well in many of them at the first rebellion raised against me,[115] which compelled me to make a great alteration among my servants. And yet the example of that corruption made me to be long troubled thereafter with solicitors recommending servants unto me more for serving in effect their friends that put them in than their master that admitted them. Let my example then teach you to follow the rules here set down, choosing your servants for your own use and not for the use of others. And since ye must be *communis parens*[116] to all your people, so choose your servants indifferently out of all quarters, not

---

[112]goods of fortune

[113]chance; Craigie notes (*Basilikon Doron* 2.230) that James had some trouble in 1603 with regard to rewarding people who had served him before his ascension to the English throne. However, both the royal holograph and the 1599 Waldegrave versions of *Basilikon Doron* contain the same reference, thus suggesting that the trouble with royal servants began prior to 1603.

[114]to forfeit, that is, to impose the sentence of forfeiture on; a forfeit is a penalty for a breach of contract or neglect, a fine or a thing lost owing to a crime or fault; James is probably referring to Bothwell indirectly here (see notes 13 and 143).

[115]James is referring to the Ruthven Raid (August 22, 1582) in which the Earl of Gowrie, a well-known ultra-Protestant, kidnapped James, who was then only 16 years old. The event deeply traumatized James. See note 109.

[116]common father or parent; see Cicero, *Tusculan Orations* 5.13.37.

respecting other men's appetites but their own qualities. For as ye must command all, so reason would ye should be served out of all as ye please to make choice.

But specially take good heed to the choice of your servants that ye prefer to the offices of the crown and estate, for in other offices ye have only to take heed to your own weal, but these concern likewise the weal of your people, for the which ye must be answerable to God. Choose then for all these offices men of known wisdom, honesty, and good conscience, well practiced in the points of the craft that ye ordain them for and free of all factions and partialities, but specially free of that filthy vice of flattery, the pest of all princes and wrack of republics. For since in the first part of this treatise I forewarned you to be at war with your own inward flatterer, *philautia*,[117] how much more should ye be at war with outward flatterers, who are nothing so sib[118] to you as your self is, by the selling of such counterfeit wares only pressing to ground their greatness upon your ruins? And therefore be careful to prefer none, as ye will be answerable to God, but only for their worthiness. But specially choose honest, diligent, mean,[119] but responsal[120] men to be your receivers in money matters. Mean I say, that ye may, when ye please, take a sharp account of their intromission[121] without peril of their breeding any trouble to your estate, for this oversight hath been the greatest cause of my misthriving in money matters.[122] Especially put never a foreigner in any principal office of estate, for that will

---

[117] in Greek letters in the original

[118] related by blood (as in "sibling")

[119] not of high rank; Craigie notes that in Anthony Weldon's *Court and Character of James I* (1651), Weldon says, "[James] ever desired to prefer mean men in great places, that when he turned them out again, they should have no friend to bandy [take sides with] them" (*Basilikon Doron* 2.231; modernized).

[120] responsible

[121] dealing

[122] Many accounts of James's difficulties with money, especially his extravagance and tendency to indebtedness, are described in David Willson's *King James VI and I;* one such account, made by M. Fontenay, the brother of Mary Queen of Scots' French secretary, reports that "The King is extremely penurious. To his domestic servants—of whom he has but a fraction of the number that served his mother—he owes more than 20,000 marks for wages and for the food and goods they have provided. He lives only by borrowing" (cited in Willson 54).

never fail to stir up sedition and envy in the countrymen's hearts, both against you and him. But (as I said before) if God provide you with more countries than this, choose the born-men of every country to be your chief counsellors therein.

And for conclusion of my advice anent the choice of your servants, delight to be served with men of the noblest blood that may be had, for besides that their service shall breed you great goodwill and least envy, contrary to that of start-ups,[123] ye shall oft find virtue follow[s] noble races, as I have said before, speaking of the nobility.

Now as to the other point anent your governing of your servants when ye have chosen them, make your court and company to be a pattern of godliness and all honest virtues to all the rest of the people. Be a daily watchman over your servants that they obey your laws precisely. For how can your laws be kept in the country if they be broken at your ear? [Punish][124] the breach thereof in a courtier more severely than in the person of any other of your subjects, and above all, suffer none of them (by abusing their credit with you) to oppress or wrong any of your subjects. Be homely[125] or strange with them as ye think their behaviour deserveth and their nature may bear with. Think a quarrelous man a pest in your company. Be careful ever to prefer the gentlest natured and trustiest to the inwardest offices about you, especially in your chalmer.[126] Suffer none about you to meddle in any men's particulars, but like the Turk's janissaries,[127] let them know no father but you, nor particular but yours. And if any will meddle in their kin or friends' quarrels, give them their leave,[128] for since ye must be of no surname nor kin but equal to all honest men, it becometh you not to be followed with partial or factious servants. Teach obedience to your servants and not to think themselves overwise, and as when any of them deserveth it ye must not spare to put them away, so without a seen cause change none of them. Pay them as all others your subjects, with *praemium* or *poena* as they

---

[123] upstarts; see Shakespeare's *Much Ado About Nothing* I.iii.66–67, for a similar use of "start-up."

[124] "Punishing" in the original

[125] intimate

[126] chamber

[127] Turkish elite infantry; a possible variant here could be Turks', the original reading "Turkes."

[128] dismiss them

deserve, which is the very ground-stone of good government. Employ every man as ye think him qualified, but use not one in all things,[129] lest he wax proud and be envied of his fellows. Love them best that are plainest with you and disguise not the truth for all their kin. Suffer none to be evil-tongued nor backbiters of them they hate. Command a heartly and brotherly love among all them that serve you. And shortly, maintain peace in your court, banish envy, cherish modesty, banish deboshed[130] insolence, foster humility, and repress pride, setting down such a comely and honourable order in all the points of your service that when strangers shall visit your court they may, with the Queen of Sheba, admire your wisdom in the glory of your house and comely order among your servants.[131]

But the principal blessing that ye can get of good company will stand in your marrying of a godly and virtuous wife, for she must be nearer unto you than any other company, being "flesh of your flesh and bone of your bone," as Adam said of Eve.[132] And because I know not but God may call me before ye be ready for marriage, I will shortly set down to you here my advice therein.

First of all consider that marriage is the greatest earthly felicity or misery that can come to a man, according as it pleaseth God to bless or curse the same. Since, then, without the blessing of God ye cannot look for a happy success in marriage, ye must be careful both in your preparation for it and in the choice and usage of your wife to procure the same. By your preparation I mean that ye must keep your body clean and unpolluted till ye give it to your wife, whom to only it belongeth. For how can ye justly crave to be joined with a pure virgin if your body be polluted? Why should the one half be clean and the other defiled? And although I know fornication is thought but a light and a venial sin by the most part of the world, yet remember well what I said to you in my first book anent conscience, and count every sin and breach of God's law not according as the vain world esteemeth of it but as God, the judge and maker of the law, accounteth of the same. Hear God commanding, by the mouth of Paul, to "abstain from fornication," declaring that the "fornicator shall not

---

[129]do not give too many responsibilities to one servant; do not give preferential treatment to one over another
[130]debauched
[131]See 1 Kings 10:8
[132]Genesis 2:23

inherit the kingdom of heaven";[133] and, by the mouth of John, reckoning out fornication amongst other grievous sins that debar the committers amongst "dogs and swine from entry into that spiritual and heavenly Jerusalem."[134] And consider, if a man shall once take upon him to count that light which God calleth heavy and venial that which God calleth grievous, beginning first to measure any one sin by the rule of his lust and appetites and not of his conscience, what shall let him to do so with the next that his affections shall stir him to, the like reason serving for all, and so to go forward till he place his whole corrupted affections in God's room? And then what shall come of him but, as a man given over to his own filthy affections, shall perish into them? And because we are all of that nature that sibbest[135] examples touch us nearest, consider the difference of success that God granted in the marriages of the king my grandfather and me your own father: the reward of his incontinency (proceeding from his evil education) being the sudden death at one time of two pleasant young princes, and a daughter only born to succeed to him, whom he had never the hap so much as once to see or bless before his death, leaving a double curse behind him to the land: both a woman of sex and a new-born babe of age to reign over them.[136] And as for the blessing God hath bestowed on me in granting me both a greater continency and the fruits following thereupon, yourself and sib folks to you[137] are (praise be to God) sufficient witnesses, which I hope the same God of his infinite mercy shall continue and increase without repentance to me and my posterity. Be not ashamed, then, to keep clean "your body, which is the

---

[133] 1 Corinthians 6:9–18

[134] Revelation 22:14–15

[135] related most closely by blood; superlative of "sib"

[136] James is referring to James (1540–41?) and Arthur (1541) dead at five days old. Apparently the two princes died within six hours of each other. The daughter to whom he refers is Mary Queen of Scots (born December 2, 1542), whose father, James V, died six days after her birth.

[137] See Craigie's note on this: "at the time of the composition of *Basilicon Doron* there were in King James's family, besides Prince Henry himself, Princess Elizabeth, born 15th August 1596, who later married the Elector Palatine of the Rhine, and Princess Margaret, born 24th December 1598. By 1603 his family had been further increased by Prince Charles, born 19th November 1600, but Princess Margaret was no longer alive, having died in infancy. Another son, Robert, born in April or May 1601, had also died in infancy" (*Basilikon Doron* 2.233).

temple of the Holy Spirit,"[138] notwithstanding all vain allurements to the contrary, discerning truly and wisely of every virtue and vice according to the true qualities thereof and not according to the vain conceits of men.

As for your choice in marriage, respect chiefly the three causes wherefore marriage was first ordained by God, and then join three accessories, so far as they may be obtained, not derogating to the principals.

The three causes it was ordained for are for staying of lust, for procreation of children, and that man should by his wife get a helper like himself.[139] Defer not then to marry till your age, for it is ordained for quenching the lust of your youth. Especially a king must timously marry for the weal of his people. Neither marry ye for any accessory cause or worldly respects a woman unable, either through age, nature, or accident, for procreation of children; for in a king that were a double fault, as well against his own weal as against the weal of his people. Neither also marry one of known evil conditions or vicious education, for the woman is ordained to be a helper, and not a hinderer, to man.

The three accessories which, as I have said, ought also to be respected without derogating to the principal causes are beauty, riches, and friendship by alliance, which are all blessings of God. For beauty increaseth your love to your wife, contenting you the better with her, without caring for others, and riches and great alliance do both make her the abler to be a helper unto you. But if over-great respect being had to these accessories, the principal causes be overseen[140] (which is overoft practiced in the world), as of themselves they are a blessing being well used, so the abuse of them will turn them in a curse. For what can all these worldly respects avail when a man shall find himself coupled with a devil, to be one flesh with him and the half-marrow in his bed? Then (though too late) shall he find that beauty without bounty, wealth without wisdom, and great friendship without grace and honesty are but fair shows and the deceitful masques of infinite miseries.

---

[138]The phrase is not quoted in italics in the original, despite it being a direct quotation from 1 Corinthians 6:19.

[139]For more on the varied causes and accessories relating to marriage, see Craigie's note (*Basilikon Doron* 2.233–34).

[140]overlooked

But have ye respect, my son, to these three special causes in your marriage, which flow from the first institution therof, *"et caetera omnia adjicientur vobis."*[141] And therefore I would rathest have you to marry one that were fully of your own religion, her rank and other qualities being agreeable to your estate. For although that to my great regret the number of any princes of power and account professing our religion be but very small, and that therefore this advice seems to be the more strait and difficile, yet ye have deeply to weigh and consider upon these doubts how ye and your wife can be of one flesh and keep unity betwixt you being members of two opposite churches. Disagreement in religion bringeth ever with it disagreement in manners, and the dissension betwixt your preachers and hers will breed and foster a dissension among your subjects, taking their example from your family, besides the peril of the evil education of your children. Neither pride you that ye will be able to frame and make her as ye please; that deceived Solomon, the wisest king that ever was, the grace of perseverance not being a flower that groweth in our garden.[142]

Remember also that marriage is one of the greatest actions that a man doth in all his time, especially in taking of his first wife; and if he marry first basely beneath his rank, he will ever be the less accounted of thereafter. And lastly, remember to choose your wife as I advised you to choose your servants: that she be of a whole and clean race, not subject to the hereditary sicknesses either of the soul or the body. For if a man will be careful to breed horses and dogs of good kinds, how much more careful should he be for the breed of his own loins? So shall ye in your marriage have respect to your conscience, honour, and natural weal in your successors.

---

[141]Matthew 6:33: "and all these things shall be added unto you." The full verse reads, "But seek ye first the kingdom of God, and his righteousness; and all these things shall be added unto you." The Vulgate text reads: *"Et haec omnia ...."*

[142]1 Kings 11:4: "It came to pass, when Solomon was old, that his wives turned away his heart after other gods." The comment suggests that it is better not to persist in being deceived like Solomon and is designed to show the firmness of James's faith in God, as opposed to that of Solomon's. The French translation of *Basilikon Doron* (1603), translates the phrase as *"à la verité le don de persévérance est de Dieu, non pas de nous"* (in truth, the gift of perseverance comes from God, not from us).

When ye are married, keep inviolably your promise made to God in your marriage, which standeth all in doing of one thing and abstaining from another: to treat her in all things as your wife and the half of yourself, and to make your body (which then is no more yours but properly hers) common with none other. I trust I need not to insist here to dissuade you from the filthy vice of adultery. Remember only what solemn promise ye make to God at your marriage, and since it is only by the force of that promise that your children succeed to you, which otherwise they could not do, equity and reason would ye should keep your part thereof. God is ever a severe avenger of all perjuries, and it is no oath made in jest that giveth power to children to succeed to great kingdoms. Have the king my grandfather's example before your eyes, who by his adultery bred the wrack of his lawful daughter and heir in begetting that bastard who unnaturally rebelled and procured the ruin of his own sovereign and sister. And what good her posterity hath gotten sensyne of some of that unlawful generation, Bothwell his treacherous attempts can bear witness.[143] Keep precisely then your promise made at marriage, as ye would wish to be partaker of the blessing therein.

And for your behaviour to your wife, the Scripture can best give you counsel therein. Treat her as your own flesh, command her as her lord, cherish her as your helper, rule her as your pupil, and please her in all things reasonable; but teach her not to be curious in things that belong [to] her not. Ye are the head; she is your body. It is your office to command and hers to obey, but yet with such a sweet harmony as she should be as ready to obey as ye to command, as willing to follow as ye to go before, your love being wholly knit unto her and all her affections lovingly bent to follow your will.

---

[143]James V, James's grandfather, was father of the illegitimate James Stewart, Earl of Moray, who was one of the leaders of the rebellion against his half-sister, Mary Queen of Scots. James V was also father of the illegitimate John Stewart, who married Lady Jane Hepburn, sister of James Hepburn, the Earl of Bothwell who was Mary's ruinous third husband. John Stewart and Jane Hepburn were the parents of Francis Stewart, the Earl of Bothwell who led a rebellion against James himself in 1591. Until Henry, James's son (and the addressee of *Basilikon Doron*), was born in 1593, this latter Bothwell could claim to be heir to the throne. His possible involvement in the witchraft trials at North Berwick includes speculation that he was actually the leader of the coven. When he died in Naples, he was reputed to be a powerful sorcerer. See the note in Craigie's *Basilikon Doron* 2.236.

And to conclude, keep specially three rules with your wife: first, suffer her never to meddle with the politic government of the commonweal but hold her at the economic rule of the house, and yet all to be subject to your direction; keep carefully good and chaste company about her, for women are the frailest sex;[144] and be never both angry at once, but when ye see her in passion, ye should with reason daunton yours, for both when ye are settled, ye are meetest to judge of her errors, and when she is come to herself, she may be best made to apprehend her offence and reverence your rebuke.

If God send you succession, be careful for their virtuous education; love them as ye ought, but let them know as much of it as the gentleness of their nature will deserve, containing them ever in a reverent love and fear of you. And in case it please God to provide[145] you to all these three kingdoms, make your eldest son Isaac,[146] leaving him all your kingdoms, and provide the rest with private possessions. Otherwise by dividing your kingdoms, ye shall leave the seed of division and discord among your posterity, as befell to this isle by the division and assignment thereof to the three sons of Brutus: Locrine, Albanact, and Camber.[147] But if God give you not

---

[144]In its treatment of women, this passage makes use of a number of classical commonplaces on the nature of women, this last being perhaps the most notable instance. See Aristotle's *Nichomachean Ethics* 8.7.1158b, for a description of the relationship between husband and wife in terms of a superior to an inferior, and his *Politics* 1.1259b, for his assertion that "the male is by nature fitter for command than the female." In James's *Dæmonologie* 2.5, James locates the Biblical source for the bias against women, stating that "as that sex is frailer than man is, so is it easier to be entrapped in these gross snares of the devil, as was overwell proved to be true by the serpent's deceiving of Eve" (*Workes* 116; modernized).

[145]advance to a position of greater importance (used, almost always, in reference to ecclesiastical promotion)

[146]See Genesis 25:5: "And Abraham gave all that he had unto Isaac."

[147]See Geoffrey of Monmouth's *Historia Regum Brittaniae* (*History of the Kings of Britain* [c. 1139]) for an account of the early Arthurian history relating to Brutus, who discovered the island of Albion and renamed it Britain after himself (1.16). Geoffrey's romance tells the story not only of the division of Britain among Brutus's three sons after his death (2.1–6), with Albanact, the youngest, getting Scotland, but also the story of King Lear's unsuccessful divestment of his kingdom among his three daughters (2.11–14). Brutus has a place in the many (and oftentimes anxiety-ridden) father-son configurations that James uses in his political and personal symbologies, not only as an example of a succession that

succession, defraud never the nearest by right, whatsoever conceit[148] ye have of the person. For kingdoms are ever at God's disposition, and in that case we are but live-renters, [it] lying no more in the king's nor people's hands to dispossess the righteous heir.[149]

And as your company should be a pattern to the rest of the people, so should your person be a lamp and mirror to your company, giving light to your servants to walk in the path of virtue and representing unto them such worthy qualities as they should press to imitate.

I need not to trouble you with the particular discourse of the four cardinal virtues,[150] it is so trodden a path. But I will shortly say unto you, make one of them, which is temperance, queen of all the rest within you.[151] I mean not by the vulgar interpretation of temperance,

---

fails but as an example of a son who killed both his own father (unwittingly in a hunting expedition) and his mother (at birth). See Craigie's note (*Basilikon Doron* 2.238–39).

[148] opinion

[149] A "live-renter" is a person with a life interest in an estate. A live-renter could administer and receive income from the estate during his lifetime but could not sell the land. In other words, kings (and the people) are but "live" tenants in terms of God's disposition of kingdoms through divinely sanctioned successions, and cannot "dispossess the righteous heir" because to do so would be to disrupt the relationship between the "rentaller" (the king or the people) and the proprietor (God). James is hinting at his relationship to Elizabeth I, and to his right to ascend to the English throne. The anxiety about succession marks both *The True Law* and *Basilikon Doron*, both of which are indefatigable in their arguments about kingship and heredity. For further commentary on this see David Harris Willson, "A Prize Much Coveted," *King James VI and I*, 138–58. One of the notable opponents to hereditary succession was the English Jesuit, Robert Parsons, who wrote under the name R. Doleman and who argued that hereditary right, in and of itself, was insufficient to guarantee succession. James's counter-argument was that "Hereditary right … was God's method of selecting kings; the right of the lawful heir was inalienable and indefeasible, and to him the people were bound as to the ruling sovereign" (Willson 140–41).

[150] justice, prudence, temperance, fortitude; see Cicero's *De Inventione* 2.53–55 and *De Officiis* 1.15–17.

[151] Cicero's *De Officiis* 3.6.28 argues that the queen of the virtues is justice. This is yet another example of James's pedantry in relation to the textual contrivances that support his arguments about kingship. Subtle revisions of classical sources perform two functions simultaneously: they bring the intertextual weight of authority to the argument; but in the subtle revisions, such as the one noted here, they show the power of kingship to depart from the traditions of that authority.

which only consists in *gustu et tactu*,[152] by the moderating of these two senses. But I mean of that wise moderation that, first commanding yourself, shall as a queen command all the affections and passions of your mind, and as a physician wisely mix all your actions according thereto. Therefore, not only in all your affections and passions but even in your most virtuous actions make ever moderation to be the chief ruler; for although holiness be the first and most requisite quality of a Christian, as proceeding from a feeling fear and true knowledge of God, yet ye remember how, in the conclusion of my first book, I advised you to moderate all your outward actions flowing therefrom. The like say I now of justice, which is the greatest virtue that properly belongeth to a king's office.

Use justice, but with such moderation as it turn not in[to] tyranny; otherwise *summum jus* is *summa injuria*.[153] As for example if a man of a known honest life be invaded by brigands or thieves for his purse and in his own defence slay one of them, they being both more in number and also known to be debauched and insolent livers, where by the contrary he was single alone, being a man of sound reputation, yet because they were not at the horn[154] or there was no eyewitness present that could verify their first invading of him, shall he therefore lose his head? And likewise, by the law-borrows[155] in our laws men are prohibited under great pecunial[156] pains from any ways invading or molesting their neighbour's person or bounds, if then his horse

---

[152] taste and touch; see Aristotle's *Nichomachean Ethics* 3.10.1118a: "Temperance and self-indulgence, however, are concerned with the kind of pleasures that the other animals share in, which therefore appear slavish and brutish; these are touch and taste."

[153] highest justice; highest injustice. The phrase occurs in Cicero's *De Officiis,* 1.10.33, and is used in *The True Law*: "And where he [the king] sees the law doubtsome or rigorous, he may interpret or mitigate the same, lest otherwise *summum jus* be *summa injuria*."

[154] outlawed; Craigie notes that "[t]he expression ['they were not at the horn'] comes from the Scots ceremony of pronouncing sentence of outlawry, in which three blasts were blown on the horn by the king's messenger" (*Basilikon Doron* 2.241).

[155] a term from Scottish law meaning the legal security required from a person that he or she will not injure the person, family, or property of another; security of the peace; to swear a law-borrows against a person is to make an affidavit of being in danger from that person.

[156] pecuniary; consisting of money

break the halter and pasture in his neighbour's meadow, shall he pay two or three thousand pounds for the wantonness of his horse or the weakness of his halter? Surely no, for laws are ordained as rules of virtuous and social living and not to be snares to trap your good subjects. And therefore the law must be interpreted according to the meaning and not to the literal sense thereof: *nam ratio est anima legis*.[157]

And as I said of justice, so say I of clemency, magnanimity, liberality, constancy, humility, and all other princely virtues, *nam in medio stat virtus*.[158] And it is but the craft of the devil that falsely coloureth the two vices that are on either side thereof with the borrowed titles of it, albeit in very deed they have no affinity therewith, and the two extremities themselves, although they seem contrary, yet growing to the height, run ever both in one. For *in infinitis omnia concurrunt*,[159] and what difference is betwixt extreme tyranny, delighting to destroy all mankind, and extreme slackness of punishment, permitting every man to tyrannize over his companion? Or what[160] differeth extreme prodigality, by wasting of all to possess nothing, from extreme niggardness, by hoarding up all to enjoy nothing, like the ass that carrying victual[s] on her back is like to starve for hunger and will be glad of thrissels[161] for her part? And what is betwixt the pride of a glorious Nebuchadnezzar[162] and the preposterous humility of one of the proud Puritans, claiming to their parity and crying, "We are all but vile worms,"[163] and yet will judge and give law to their king but will be judged nor controlled by none? Surely there is more pride under such a one's black bonnet than under

---

[157] for reason is the spirit [soul] of the law; the phrase adapts Cicero's *lex est ratio summa* or "law is the highest reason" (*De Legibus* 1.6.18).

[158] for virtue stands in the mean; see Aristotle's *Nichomachean Ethics* 2.6.1107a, although as Craigie indicates, it is more likely that James intends the phrase in the context of virtue as the mean between two vices (*Basilikon Doron* 2.241).

[159] in the infinite all things meet

[160] in the sense of "how"

[161] thistles

[162] Nebuchadnezzar was king of Babylon during the last Babylonian empire, marked by its extensive trade, architecture, art, astronomy and military might. He conquered Jerusalem in 597 BCE. See Daniel 4:30 for the specific Scriptural passage of which James may have been thinking.

[163] See Job 25:5–6

Alexander the Great his diadem,[164] as was said of Diogenes in the like case.[165]

But above all virtues, study to know well your own craft, which is to rule your people. And when I say this, I bid you know all crafts; for except ye know every one, how can ye control every one, which is your proper office? Therefore besides your education, it is necessary ye delight in reading and seeking the knowledge of all lawful things, but with these two restrictions: first, that ye choose idle hours for it, not interrupting therewith the discharge of your office; and next, that ye study not for knowledge nakedly, but that your principal end be to make you able thereby to use your office, practicing according to your knowledge in all the points of your calling not like these vain astrologians[166] that study night and day on the course of the stars only that they may, for satisfying their curiosity, know their course. But since all arts and sciences are linked every one with [the] other, their greatest principles agreeing in one (which moved the poets to feign[167] the nine Muses to be all sisters), study them that out of their harmony ye may suck the knowledge of all faculties, and consequently be on the council of all crafts, that ye may be able to

---

[164]crown

[165]Alexander the Great (356–323 BCE) was a student of Aristotle's and leader of a military monarchy that extended Greek influence throughout the east, thus radically changing the nature of the Greek city-state. Diogenes (4th century BCE) was an important exponent of the Cynic school of philosophy (founded circa 440 BCE by Antisthenes) that argued virtue was the basis of happiness and could be achieved through freedom from desire: in Diogenes' time cynicism involved contempt for both knowledge and accepted morality. A reputed meeting between Alexander and Diogenes at Corinth in which Alexander, seeing Diogenes lying in the sun, asked if he could do anything for Diogenes. Diogenes responded by telling Alexander not to block the sun, to which Alexander replied that if he were not Alexander he would wish to be Diogenes. James is making the tendentious argument that the Puritan, like Diogenes, has more pride than Alexander. James seems to have had a fondness for such stories relating the insolence of philosophers and poets to kings and tyrants as evidenced in his citation in Book Three of *Basilikon Doron* of Philoxenus's reply to Dionysius the Younger.

[166]astronomers; see Craigie's long note on the distinction between astronomers and astrologians, something to which James had addressed himself in the fourth chapter of the first book of *Dæmonologie* (*Basilikon Doron* 2.242–43).

[167]imagine or conceive of

contain them all in order, as I have already said; for knowledge and learning [are][168] a light burden, the weight whereof will never press your shoulders.

First of all, then, study to be well seen in the Scriptures, as I remembered you in the first book, as well for the knowledge of your own salvation as that ye may be able to contain your church in their calling, as *custos utriusque tabulae*.[169] For the ruling them well is no small point of your office, taking specially heed that they[170] vague[171] not from their text in the pulpit. And if ever ye would have peace in your land, suffer them not to meddle in that place with the estate or policy, but punish severely the first that presumeth to it.[172] Do nothing towards them without a good ground and warrant, but reason not much with them, for I have overmuch surfeited them with that, and it is not their fashion to yield. And suffer no conventions nor meetings among churchmen but by your knowledge and permission.[173]

Next[174] the Scriptures study well your own laws, for how can ye discern by the thing ye know not? But press to draw all your laws and processes to be as short and plain as ye can; assure yourself the longsomeness[175] both of rights and processes[176] breedeth their un-

---

[168] "is" in the original

[169] guardian of each tablet; see Exodus 34 for a description of the Decalogue and the two tablets on which the moral and religious duties of the ten commandments—brought down by Moses from Mount Sinai—were inscribed. The side-note in the original makes reference to Deuteronomy 17, James (or his printer) probably having in mind verses 14 and 15: "When thou art come unto the land which the Lord thy God giveth thee, and shalt possess it, and shalt dwell therein, and shalt say, I will set a king over me, like as all the nations that are about me; Thou shalt in any wise set him king over thee, whom the Lord thy God shall choose: one from among thy brethren shalt thou set king over thee: thou mayest not set a stranger over thee, which is not thy brother."

[170] James is referring to ministers of the kirk throughout this paragraph.

[171] wander

[172] In April 1593, the General Assembly of the kirk met and, by an Act of Assembly requested by James, ordered ministers not to speak from the pulpit against the king, his council, or the proceedings of both.

[173] Conventions and meetings of churchmen were disallowed (without royal consent) by an Act of Parliament in 1584.

[174] next to

[175] repetitiousness

[176] "rights and processes" in this context refers to laws and legal proceedings;

sure looseness and obscurity, the shortest being ever both the surest
and plainest form and the longsomeness serving only for the enrich-
ing of the advocates and clerks with the spoil of the whole country.
And therefore delight to haunt your session and spy carefully their
proceedings, taking good heed if any bribery may be tried among
them, which cannot overseverely be punished. Spare not to go there,
for gracing that far any that ye favour by your presence to procure
them expedition of justice, although that should be specially done
for the poor that cannot wait on or are debarred by mightier parties.
But when ye are there, remember the throne is God's and not yours
that ye sit in, and let no favour nor whatsoever respects move you
from the right. Ye sit not there, as I show before, for rewarding of
friends or servants, nor for crossing of contemners,[177] but only for
doing of justice. Learn also wisely to discern betwixt justice and
equity, and for pity of the poor rob not the rich because he may better
spare it, but give the little man the larger coat if it be his, eschewing
the error of young Cyrus[178] therein. For justice, by the law, giveth

---

in this passage James is criticizing the repetitious diction and rhetoric that
characterized Scottish Acts of Parliament and the length of trials.

[177] despisers, scorners

[178] Cyrus the Great (d. 529 BCE) founded the Persian empire. Xenophon, an
Athenian who knew Socrates, wrote the *Cyropaedia* ("Education of Cyrus"),
which tells the story of Cyrus's career. The *Cyropaedia*, generally understood to be
an historical romance and not a "true" biographical or historical account of Cyrus's
life, is one of the classical models that James uses to derive ideas about the quality
of kingship and statecraft expected of Henry in the *Basilikon Doron*. The incident
with the coat to which James is referring occurs in *Cyropaedia* 1.3.16–17. Cyrus
explains how he received a whipping for misjudgment after being asked by his
master to try a case: "There were two boys, a big boy and a little boy, and the big
boy's coat was small and the small boy's coat was huge. So the big boy stripped the
little boy and gave him his own small coat, while he put on the big one himself. Now
in giving judgment I decided that it was better for both parties that each should have
the coat that fitted him best. But I never got any further in my sentence, because the
master thrashed me here, and said that the verdict would have been excellent if I
had been appointed to say what fitted and what did not, but I had been called in to
decide to whom the coat belonged, and the point to consider was, who had a right
to it: Was he who took a thing by violence to keep it, or he who had had it made
and bought it for his own? And the master taught me that what is lawful is just and
what is in the teeth of the law is based on violence, and therefore, he said, the
judge must always see that his verdict tallies with the law" (15–16), in Xenophon,

every man his own, and equity in things arbitral[179] giveth everyone that which is meetest for him.

Be an ordinary sitter in your secret council;[180] that judicature is only ordained for matters of estate and repressing of insolent oppressions. Make that judgement as compendious and plain as ye can, and suffer no advocates to be heard there with their dilators,[181] but let every party tell his own tale himself, and weary not to hear the complaints of the oppressed, *aut ne rex sis*.[182] Remit everything to the ordinary judicature for eschewing of confusion, but let it be your own craft to take a sharp account of every man in his office.

And next the laws I would have you to be well-versed in authentic histories and in the chronicles of all nations, but specially in our own histories (*ne sis peregrinus domi*),[183] the example whereof most nearly concerns you. I mean not of such infamous invectives as Buchanan's or Knox's chronicles;[184] and if any of these infamous libels remain until your days, use the law upon the keepers thereof. For in that point I would have you a Pythagorist[185] to think that the very spirits of these archibellouses[186] of rebellion have made transition in them that [hoard][187] their books or [maintain][188] their opinions, punishing them even as it were their authors risen again. But by reading of authentic histories and chronicles, ye shall learn experi-

---

The Education of Cyrus, tr. H. G. Dakyns (London: J. M. Dent, 1992).

[179]discretionary

[180]the Privy Council, consisting of the sovereign's private counsellors

[181]delays

[182]or do not be king; see Plutarch's *Life of Demetrius* 42.3

[183]indeed do not be a foreigner at home

[184]James is referring to George Buchanan's *Rerum Scoticarum Historia,* published in 1592, and to John Knox's *Historie of the Reformation,* never published during Knox's lifetime (its first three books were printed in 1587, but before publication most copies were destroyed by order of the Archbishop of Canterbury).

[185]Pythagorean; Pythagoras is the sixth century BCE Greek philosopher who believed in the transmigration of souls. James wants Henry to understand that, in a manner similar to Pythagoras's belief in transmigration, hoarders of books and opinions associated with rebellion are in fact sustaining the spirit of those original inciters to rebellion (in this case, Buchanan and Knox).

[186]extreme inciters

[187]"hoardes" in original

[188]"maintaines" in original

ence by theoric, applying the by-past things to the present estate, *quia nihil novum sub sole;*[189] such is the continual volubility[190] of things earthly, according to the roundness of the world and revolution of the heavenly circles, which is expressed by the wheels in Ezekiel's visions[191] and counterfeited by the poets *in rota fortunæ.*[192] And likewise by the knowledge of histories, ye shall know how to behave yourself to all ambassadors and strangers, being able to discourse with them upon the estate of their own country. And among all profane histories, I must not omit most specially to recommend unto you the *Commentaries* of Cæsar, both for the sweet flowing of the style as also for the worthiness of the matter itself.[193] For I have ever been of that opinion that of all the ethnic[194] emperors or great captains that ever were, he hath farthest excelled both in his practice and in his precepts in martial affairs.

As for the study of other liberal arts and sciences, I would have you reasonably versed in them, but not pressing to be a past-master[195] in any of them, for that cannot but distract you from the points of your calling as I showed you before. And when, by the enemy winning the town, ye shall be interrupted in your demonstration, as Archimedes was,[196] your people (I think) will look very bluntly upon

---

[189]because "there is no new thing beneath the sun"; see Ecclesiastes 1:9

[190]turning on axis

[191]Ezekiel 1:15–21

[192]in the wheel of Fortune

[193]Julius Caesar's *Commentaries* relate the events of the Gallic and Civil wars in which he was engaged. Book 1, chapter 11 of *The Book Named the Governor* (1531) by Sir Thomas Elyot recommends the study of the *Commentaries.*

[194]heathen; James mentions "Ethnike Princes" in his 1609 work *A Premonition to All Most Mightie Monarches, Kings, Free Princes, and States of Christendome* (*Workes* 296). *A Premonition* was a lengthy defence of "the authority and privilege of kings in general and all supereminent temporal powers" (*Workes* 289; modernized) against the accusation by Robert Bellarmine, a well-known Catholic controversialist, that the Oath of Allegiance was merely civil. For more on this controversy see McIlwain, particularly xlix-lxii.

[195]expert

[196]James is warning Henry of the dangers of being too absorbed in one's studies, something Shakespeare uses as a motif to explain Prospero's deposition as Duke of Milan in *The Tempest*:

> And Prospero the prime duke, being so reputed
> In dignity, and for the liberal arts

it. I grant it is meet ye have some entrance, specially in the mathematics, for the knowledge of the art military: in situation of camps, ordering of battles, making fortifications, placing of batteries, or suchlike.[197] And let not this your knowledge be dead without fruits, as Saint James speaketh of faith,[198] but let it appear in your daily conversation and in all the actions of your life.

Embrace true magnanimity, not in being vindictive, which the corrupted judgements of the world think to be true magnanimity, but by the contrary, in thinking your offender not worthy of your wrath, empiring over your own passion and triumphing in the commanding yourself to forgive, husbanding the effects of your courage and wrath to be rightly employed upon repelling of injuries within by revenge taking upon the oppressors and in revenging injuries without by just wars upon foreign enemies. And so, where ye find a notable injury, spare not to give course to the torrents of your wrath. "The wrath of a king is like to the roaring of a lion."[199]

Foster true humility in banishing pride, not only towards God (considering ye differ not in stuff but in use, and that only by his ordinance, from the basest of your people) but also towards your parents. And if it fall out that my wife shall outlive me, as ever ye

---

Without a parallel; those being all my study,
The government I cast upon my brother,
And to my state grew stranger, being transported
And rapt in secret studies. (I.ii.72–77)

Archimedes, the great inventor and mathematician from Syracuse (third century BCE, circa 287–212), was killed, according to Plutarch (*Life of Marcellus* 19.4), when he refused to obey a soldier because he was so taken up with a mathematical problem.

[197]See Shakespeare's *Othello*, I.i.19–26. Iago complains about having been passed over for promotion by

a great arithmetician,
One Michael Cassio, a Florentine....
That never set a squadron in the field,
Nor the division of a battle knows
More than a spinster—unless the bookish theoric,
Wherein the toged consuls can propose
As masterly as he.

[198]James 2:17: "Even so faith, if it hath not works, is dead, being alone."

[199]Proverbs 20:2. James's 1611 Authorized Version of the Bible has a notably different translation: "The fear of a king is as the roaring of a lion."

think to purchase my blessing, honour your mother.[200] Set Bathsheba[201] in a throne on your right hand; offend her for nothing, much less wrong her. Remember her, *quæ longa decem tulerit fastidia menses*,[202] and that your flesh and blood [are] made of hers, and begin not, like the young lords and lairds,[203] your first wars upon your mother, but press earnestly to deserve her blessing. Neither deceive yourself with many that say they care not for their parents' curse so they deserve it not. O invert not the order of nature by judging your superiors, chiefly in your own particular. But assure yourself the blessing or curse of the parents hath almost ever a prophetic power joined with it, and if there were no more, honour your parents for the lengthening of your own days, as God in his law promiseth.[204] Honour also them that are *in loco parentum*[205] unto you, such as your governors,[206] upbringers, and preceptors. Be thankful unto them and reward them, which is your duty and honour.

But on the other part, let not this true humility stay your high indignation to appear when any great oppressors shall presume to come in your presence; then frown as ye ought. And in case they use a colour of law in oppressing their poor ones, as over many do, that which ye cannot mend by law mend by the withdrawing of your countenance from them. And once in the year cross them, when their errands come in your way, recompensing the oppressor according to Christ's parable of the two debtors.[207]

---

[200] In November 1598 when James married Anne of Denmark, she was just about to turn fifteen, while James was 24. She died in 1619, six years before James.

[201] Bathsheba, Solomon's mother, was formerly wife of Uriah the Hittite, whom David, Solomon's father, did away with by sending into battle. See 2 Samuel 11–12 and 1 Kings 1–2. Again, the biblical reference is designed to draw connections, however subtly, between Henry and Solomon.

[202] because ten months have brought the weariness of travail [of labour to your mother]; the phrase *longa ... menses* is directly lifted from Virgil's *Eclogues* 4.61 and occurs in the context of not making Henry's mother suffer further, since she has suffered enough during her pregnancy.

[203] landed proprietors equivalent to the English gentry

[204] See Exodus 20:12

[205] in the place or position of parents

[206] tutors; see Roger Ascham's *The Scholemaster* (1570), which makes use of the word governor in relation to the "correct[ion] of manners" as opposed to scholarship.

[207] Matthew 18:23–35. The parable tells the story of a king who forgives the debt of one of his servants only to find out that the same servant has not forgiven

Keep true constancy, not only in your kindness towards honest men but being also *invicti animi*[208] against all adversities, not with that stoic insensible stupidity wherewith many in our days, pressing to win honour in imitating that ancient sect,[209] by their inconstant behaviour in their own lives belie their profession. But although ye are not a stock, not to feel calamities, yet let not the feeling of them so overrule and dozen[210] your reason as may stay you from taking and using the best resolution for remedy that can be found out.

Use true liberality in rewarding the good and bestowing frankly for your honour and weal, but with that proportional discretion that every man may be served according to his measure, wherein respect must be had to his rank, deserts, and necessity. And provide how to have, but cast not away without cause. In special, impair not by your liberality the ordinary rents of your crown, whereby the estate royal of you and your successors must be maintained; *ne exhaurias fontem liberalitas,*[211] for that would ever be kept *sacrosanctum et extra commercium;*[212] otherwise your liberality would decline to prodigality, in helping others with your and your successors' hurt. And above all, enrich not yourself with exactions upon your subjects, but think the riches of your people your best treasure, by the sins of offenders, where no prevention can avail, making justly your commodity.[213] And in case necessity of wars or other extraordinaries compel you to

---

a debt he is owed by a fellow servant. Because of the first servant's lack of compassion, the king "delivered him to the tormentors, till he should pay all that was due unto him."

[208] of invincible spirit, courage, or character

[209] The Stoic school of philosophy, founded by Zeno in the fourth century BCE, was characterized by detachment from the material world and by the belief that the universe is absorbed into a divine fire, then reborn exactly as it was before in an infinite cycle of creation and decay. In James's day "Stoic" referred to the ancient Roman stoics and such modern editors and commentators as Justus Lipsius. The context of this passage is unclear, James possibly railing against religious dogmatism, or against the hypocrisy of his political opponents who disguise their inconstancy with a display of stoic virtue.

[210] stupify

[211] do not exhaust the source of generosity

[212] inviolable and apart from commerce

[213] The meaning and syntax of this phrase are somewhat obscure though James seems to be saying that Henry must gain advantage from those "offenders" rather than from his "subjects."

lift subsidies, do it as rarely as ye can, employing it only to the use it was ordained for and using yourself in that case as *fidus depositarius*[214] to your people.

And principally, exercise true wisdom in discerning wisely betwixt true and false reports: first, considering the nature of the person reporter; next, what entresse[215] he can have in the weal or evil of him of whom he maketh the report; thirdly, the likelihood of the purpose itself; and last, the nature and by-past life of the dilated person. And where ye find a tratler,[216] away with him. And although it be true that a prince can never without secrecy do great things, yet it is better ofttimes to try reports than by credulity to foster suspicion upon an honest man. For since suspicion is the tyrant's sickness, as the fruits of an evil conscience, *potius in alteram partem peccato,*[217] I mean, in not mistrusting one whom to no such unhonesty was known before. But as for such as have slipped before, former experience may justly breed prevention by foresight.

And to conclude my advice anent your behaviour in your person, consider that God is the author of all virtue, having imprinted in men's minds by the very light of nature the love of all moral virtues, as was seen by the virtuous lives of the old Romans, and press then to shine as far before your people in all virtue and honesty as in greatness of rank, that the use thereof in all your actions may turn with time to a natural habitude[218] in you, and as by their hearing of your laws, so by their sight of your person both their eyes and their ears may lead and allure them to the love of virtue and hatred of vice.

---

[214] trusty depositary

[215] benefit, interest

[216] idle talker

[217] better having erred in another direction; the context of this sentence, despite the obscure syntax, simply suggests it is better to err on the side of trust and honesty than on the side of suspicion and dishonesty.

[218] mental or bodily disposition, custom

Of A King's Behaviour in Indifferent Things

The Third Book

It is a true old saying "that a king is as one set on a stage, whose smallest actions and gestures all the people gazingly do behold." And therefore, although a king be never so precise in the discharging of his office, the people, who seeth but the outward part, will ever judge of the substance by the circumstances; and according to the outward appearance, if his behaviour be light or dissolute, will conceive preoccupied conceits of the king's inward intention, which although with time (the trier of all truth) it will evanish[1] by the evidence of the contrary effects, yet *interim patitur justus*;[2] and prejudged[3] conceits will in the meantime breed contempt, the mother of rebellion and disorder. And besides that, it is certain that all the indifferent[4] actions and behaviour of a man have a certain holding and dependence either upon virtue or vice, according as they are used or ruled, for there is not a middes betwixt them no more than betwixt their rewards, heaven and hell.

Be careful then, my son, so to frame all your indifferent actions and outward behaviour as they may serve for the furtherance and forth-setting of your inward virtuous disposition.

The whole indifferent actions of a man I divide in two sorts: in his behaviour in things necessary, as food, sleeping, raiment, speaking,

---

[1] perhaps as in "evanesce," fade away slowly

[2] meanwhile the just man suffers

[3] prejudiced

[4] things and actions neither good nor bad *per se,* things that do not matter in themselves but only in context or as part of larger concerns; the word "indifferent" can also in rare cases mean "different," as it may signify in James's title to this book. James uses the word throughout this book with its full range of meaning.

writing, and gesture; and in things not necessary, though convenient and lawful, as pastimes or exercises and using of company for recreation.

As to the indifferent things necessary, although that of themselves they cannot be wanted and so in that case are not indifferent, as likewise in case they be not used with moderation, declining so to the extremity, which is vice, yet the quality and form of using them may smell of virtue or vice and be great furtherers to any of them.

To begin then at the things necessary: one of the publickest[5] indifferent actions of a king, and that maniest,[6] especially strangers, will narrowly take heed to, is his manner of refection[7] at his table and his behaviour thereat. Therefore, as kings use oft to eat publicly, it is meet and honourable that ye also do so, as well to eschew the opinion that ye love not to haunt company, which is one of the marks of a tyrant,[8] as likewise that your delight to eat privately be not thought to be for private satisfying of your gluttony, which ye would be ashamed should be publicly seen. Let your table be honourably served, but serve your appetite with few dishes, as young Cyrus did,[9] which both is wholesomest and freest from the vice of delicacy, which is a degree of gluttony. And use most to eat of reasonably gross[10] and common meats, as well for making your body strong and durable for travail[11] at all occasions, either in peace or in war, as that ye may be the heartlier received by your mean subjects in their houses when their cheer may suffice you, which otherwise would be imputed to you for pride and daintiness and breed coldness and disdain in them. Let all your food be simple, without composition or sauces, which are more like medicines than meat. The using of them was counted amongst the ancient Romans a filthy vice

---

[5] most public

[6] many if not most

[7] refreshment by food or drink

[8] See Xenophon's *Cyropaedia* 8.4.1–5.

[9] James is referring to an incident in the first book of *Cyropaedia* (1.3.4–5), in which Cyrus's grandfather, Astyages, sets a rich table full of food and asks Cyrus if such a table is finer than Persian fare. Cyrus is said to have responded by arguing for a simple diet: "We are hungry and wish to be fed, and bread and meat bring us to where we want to be at once, but you, Medes, for all your haste, take so many turns and wind about so much it is a wonder if you ever find your way to the goal we have reached long ago" (*The Education of Cyrus* 12).

[10] coarse

[11] severe bodily exertion

of delicacy, because they serve only for pleasing of the taste and not for satisfying of the necessity of nature, abhorring Apicius, their own citizen, for his vice of delicacy and monstrous gluttony.[12] Like as both the Grecians and Romans had in detestation the very name of Philoxenus for his filthy wish of a crane craig.[13] And therefore was that sentence used amongst them against these artificial false appetites, *optimum condimentum fames*.[14] But beware with using excess of meat and drink, and chiefly beware of drunkenness, which is a beastly vice, namely in a king, but specially beware with it because it is one of those vices that increaseth with age. In the form of your meat-eating, be neither uncivil, like a gross Cynic, nor affectately mignard,[15] like a dainty dame, but eat in a manly, round, and honest fashion. It is no ways comely to dispatch affairs or to be pensive at

---

[12]M. Gavius Apicius was a Roman epicure who lived during Tiberius's reign. The marginal note in the original includes a reference to Juvenal's second satire, which was an extended attack on Roman effeminacy and homosexuality. No direct mention is made of Apicius in this satire, and it is possible that James, through inclusion of the note either by himself or his printer, was using this opportunity to mount an indirect attack on homosexuality, despite his own well-chronicled proclivities. For a more complete discussion of the use of the term "homosexuality" in relation to the Renaissance, see Alan Bray, *Homosexuality in Renaissance England* (London: Gay Men's Press, 1982), especially 13–19. Bray begins the book with a discussion of the translation of two Greek words with homosexual connotations in 1 Corinthians 6 by biblical scholars working on James's Authorized Version of the Bible. Bray suggests that "[t]heir translation is revealing. The first they translated as 'effeminate,' a word which then lacked the specifically homosexual connotations it was later to acquire; the second they translated by a mere description, albeit a description coloured by their disapproval: 'abusers of themselves with mankind.' More than three hundred years later, in the middle of the twentieth century, another panel of scholars considered the same passage and translated it afresh. They would need, they decided, to combine the two Greek words and translate them by a single expression, one of a different order. Both were translated in a word: 'homosexuals'" (13). Bray goes on to discuss the anachronistic usage of the term "homosexual," which "did not exist in 1611" (13), with reference to Renaissance sexual behaviours.

[13]See Athenaeus, *Deipnosophists* 1.6b, for an account of the glutton Philoxenus who wished for a crane neck in order to be able to ingest, and therefore enjoy, more food.

[14]hunger is the best seasoning; this was a variation on the notion that hunger is the best appetizer, also phrased, in the Scottish proverb, as "Hunger is good kitchen." See Craigie's note on the classical sources of this phrase (*Basilikon Doron* 2.255).

[15]affectedly dainty

meat, but keep then an open and cheerful countenance, causing to read pleasant histories unto you that profit may be mixed with pleasure, and when ye are not disposed, entertain pleasant, quick, but honest discourses.

And because meat provoketh sleeping, be also moderate in your sleep, for it goeth much by use; and remember that if your whole life were divided in four parts, three of them would be found to be consumed on meat, drink, sleep, and unnecessary occupations.

But albeit ordinary times would commonly be kept in meat and sleep, yet use[16] yourself sometimes so that any time in the four and twenty hours may be alike to you for any of them, that thereby your diet may be accomodate[17] to your affairs and not your affairs to your diet, not therefore using yourself to over-great softness and delicacy in your sleep more than in your meat, and specially in case ye have ado[18] with the wars.

Let not your chalmer be throng[19] and common in the time of your rest, as well for comeliness as for eschewing of carrying reports out of the same. Let them that have the credit to serve in your chalmer be trusty and secret, for a king will have need to use secrecy in many things, but yet behave yourself so in your greatest secrets as ye need not be ashamed suppose they were all proclaimed at the Mercat Cross.[20] But specially see that those of your chalmer be of a sound fame and without blemish.

---

[16] accustom

[17] suited

[18] action (as in to-do), business, fuss, difficulty

[19] crowded with people

[20] Mercat(e) is an obsolete word for market. The Mercat Cross is a decorated stone pulpit opposite the City Chambers along Edinburgh's Royal Mile, just below St. Giles' Cathedral. On royal occasions heralds make proclamations at the cross. The history of the cross is bloody and fascinating. James I's assassin, the Earl of Atholl, was crowned with a red hot diadem at the cross in the fifteenth century; in 1513 prior to the battle of Flodden, one Richard Lawson passed the Mercat Cross and "was amazed to hear a fanfare of trumpets sound through the plague-stricken town. Then from the Cross he listened to a ghostly voice as it recited the names of those who would fall in the coming battle, starting with that of the King" (see Sacheverell Sitwell and Francis Bamford, *Edinburgh* [London: John Lehmann, 1948], 39). An Edinburgh merchant, Birrel, who flourished during Mary's reign, the regency, and James's Scottish years, left a diary telling of a tumbler who "hitched his tight-rope to the Crown Steeple of St. Giles and performed his antics before the crowds around the Mercat Cross" (George Scott-Moncrieff, *Edinburgh*

Take no heed to any of your dreams, for all prophesies, visions, and prophetic dreams are accomplished and ceased in Christ. And therefore take no heed to freets[21] either in dreams or any other things; for that error proceedeth of ignorance and is unworthy of a Christian, who should be assured *omnia esse pura puris*, as Paul saith, all days and meats being alike to Christians.[22]

Next followeth to speak of raiment, the on-putting whereof is the ordinary action that followeth next to sleep. Be also moderate in your raiment, neither over-superfluous, like a deboshed waster,[23] nor yet over-base, like a miserable wretch; not artificially trimmed and decked, like a courtesan, nor yet over-sluggishly clothed, like a country clown; not over-lightly like a candy soldier[24] or a vain young

---

[London: B.T. Batsford, 1947], 38).

[21] superstitions

[22] "Unto the pure all things are pure" (Titus 1:15); Romans 14:20: "All things indeed are pure; but it is evil for that man who eateth with offence." James's private as opposed to his public beliefs about dreaming are of relevance here. George Nicolson, the English agent at the Scottish court, wrote that "I have heard but in great secret and so I beseech your honour [Sir William Cecil] to keep it. That .126 [a cypher for James] was troubled in his chamber in his sleep, and hath taken conceit that .200 [a cypher for Elizabeth] shall outlive him, and thereon hath he written an apology and rule how his son shall be brought to succeed .200 to that place, and how all shall be governed for the attaining thereunto .... (*Basilikon Doron* 2.4; modernized). Nonetheless, it was commonplace for Renaissance commentators to diminish the significance of dreams. For instance, Giovanni Della Casa in *Galateo,* a sixteenth-century courtesy book, states: "Those who describe their dreams in great detail and with great enthusiasm making such fuss that one is left exhausted just hearing them, behave wrongly, especially since, in most cases, it would be a waste of time to listen to the greatest achievement of this type of person, even if they had accomplished it while awake. Thus, one should not bore others with such worthless things as dreams, especially since most dreams are generally silly" (Giovanni Della Casa, *Galateo,* tr. Konrad Eisenbichler and Kenneth R. Bartlett [Toronto: CRRS, 1990], 19).

[23] a debauched ne'er-do-well; "waster" refers to one who lives in idleness or extravagance

[24] The Spanish translation of *Basilikon Doron* by Juan Pemberton (c. 1603; Scottish National Library MS. 3855) renders the phrase as "no de masiado galano, como soldado de Candia, como un vano y nuevo cortesano" (44r., ll. 4–5). In the Pemberton translation "Candia" refers to the Venetian word for Crete, for almost five centuries (from the Fourth Crusade to the surrender to the Turks of the city of Iraklion, also known as Candia, in 1699) a settlement colony of Venice, primarily because of its importance as one stopover among many (including Corfu, Methoni,

courtier, nor yet over-gravely, like a minister. But in your garments be proper, cleanly, comely, and honest, wearing your clothes in a careless yet comely form, keeping in them a mid form, *inter togatos et paludatos*,[25] betwixt the gravity of the one and lightness of the other, thereby to signify that by your calling ye are mixed of both the professions: *togatus*, as a judge making and pronouncing the law; *paludatus*, by the power of the sword, as your office is likewise mixed betwixt the ecclesiastical and civil estate. For a king is not *mere laicus*,[26] as both the Papists and Anabaptists would have him, to the which error also the Puritans incline over-far.[27] But to return to the purpose of garments, they ought to be used according to their first institution by God, which was for three causes: first, to hide our nakedness and shame; next and consequently, to make us more comely; and thirdly, to preserve us from the injuries of heat and cold. If to hide our nakedness and shameful parts, then these natural parts, ordained to be hid, should not be represented by any undecent forms in the clothes, and if they should help our comeliness, they should not then by their painted, preened fashion serve for baits to filthy lechery, as false hair and fairding[28] does amongst unchaste women; and if they should preserve us from the injuries of heat and cold, men should not, like senseless stones, contemn God in lightlying the seasons, glorying to conquer honour on heat and cold. And although it be praiseworthy and necessary in a prince to be *patiens algoris et aestus*[29] when he shall have ado with wars upon the fields, yet I think it meeter that ye go both clothed and armed than naked to the battle, except you would make you light for away-running; and yet for

---

Kithira, Cyprus, and Beirut) for Venetian ships plying their trade with the Near East, but also a favoured place of employment for impoverished Venetian nobility. It is likely that James was using the obscure form of "Candy" to refer specifically to Candia or to Crete. For further information on this term see Fischlin, "The 'Candie-souldier,' Venice, and James VI (I)'s Advice on Monarchic Dress in *Basilikon Doron*."

[25] between those wearing a toga (like a judge) and those wearing a general's coat or *paludamentum*

[26] purely a layman

[27] This was not James's only strange conflation of Catholicism with Protestant sects; McIlwain notes that "James I had himself declared [in *A Premonition* ...], 'Jesuits are nothing more than Puritan-papists'" (xxii). See McIlwain's introduction for a summary of religious positionings contemporary to James.

[28] make-up, painting of the face

[29] tolerant of cold and heat

cowards, *metus addit alas*.[30] And shortly, in your clothes keep a proportion as well with the seasons of the year as of your age, in the fashions of them being careless, using them according to the common form of the time, sometimes richlier, sometimes meanlier clothed, as occasion serveth, without keeping any precise rule therein. For if your mind be found occupied upon them, it will be thought idle otherwise, and ye shall be accounted in the number of one of these *compti juvenes*,[31] which will make your spirit and judgement to be less thought of. But specially eschew to be effeminate in your clothes, in perfuming, preening, or suchlike, and fail never in time of wars to be galliardest[32] and bravest both in clothes and countenance. And make not a fool of yourself in disguising or wearing long hair or nails, which are but excrements of nature and bewray[33] such misusers of them to be either of a vindictive or a vain light natural.[34] Especially, make no vows in such vain and outward things as concern either meat or clothes.

Let yourself and all your court wear no ordinary armour with your clothes but such as is knightly and honourable: I mean rapier-swords and daggers. For tuilyiesome[35] weapons in the court [betoken][36] confusion in the country. And therefore banish not only from your court all traitorous offensive weapons forbidden by the laws, as guns and suchlike (whereof I spake already), but also all traitorous defensive arms, as secrets,[37] plate-sleeves,[38] and suchlike unseen armour.

---

[30]This is a rephrasing of Virgil's line from the *Aeneid* (8.224), *Pedibus timor addidit alas* or "fear lent wings to his feet." James's version of it translates as "fear lends wings."

[31]arrayed like a youth; the phrase is found in Ovid's *Heroides* 4.75 as *sint procul a nobis iuvenes ut femina compti!* or "away from me with your young men arrayed like women!" Close readers of the text may find another covert reference to homosexuality here (see note 12), especially in terms of the closing lines of the paragraph.

[32]A galliard is a quick and lively dance in triple time for two persons or the music for it; it derives from *gallia* or strength, and is of Celtic origin. Here, James is probably using it in the sense of "strongest" or "liveliest." See Shakespeare's *Henry V* I.ii.251–53, in which one of the ambassadors states, "there's nought in France / That can be with a nimble galliard won; / You cannot revel into dukedoms there."

[33]show or betray

[34]disposition

[35]used for brawling; a "tuilyie" is a quarrel, brawl, fight, noisy contest or dispute

[36]"betokens" in the original

[37]coat of mail concealed under one's ordinary apparel

[38]thin pieces of steel woven together onto fabric and used to armour the sleeves

"Man of Sphakia in Crete." Woodcut from Cesare Vecellio's
Habiti antichi, et moderni di tutto il Mondo
(printed by Giovanni Bernardo Sessa, Venice 1598).

For besides that the wearers thereof may be presupposed to have a secret evil intention, they want both the uses that defensive armour is ordained for: which is to be able to hold out violence and by their outward glancing in their enemies' eyes to strike a terror in their hearts;[39] where, by the contrary, they can serve for neither, being not only unable to resist but dangerous for shots, and giving no outward show against the enemy, being only ordained for betraying under trust,[40] whereof honest men should be ashamed to bear the outward badge, not resembling the thing they are not. And for answer against these arguments I know none but the old Scots fashion, which if it be wrong, is no more to be allowed for ancientness than the old Mass is, which also our forefathers used.[41]

The next thing that ye have to take heed to is your speaking and language, whereunto I join your gesture, since action is one of the chiefest qualities that is required in an orator; for as the tongue speaketh to the ears, so doth the gesture speak to the eyes of the auditor. In both your speaking and your gesture use a natural and plain form not fairded with artifice, for (as the Frenchmen say) "*rien contrefait fin*";[42] but eschew all affectate forms in both.

In your language be plain, honest, natural, comely, clean, short, and sententious, eschewing both the extremities, as well in not using any rustical corrupt leed[43] as book language and pen and inkhorn terms,[44] and least of all mignard and effeminate terms. But let the greatest part of your eloquence consist in a natural, clear, and sensible form of the delivery of your mind, builded ever upon certain

---

[39]The idea here is that the outward show of strength that goes along with being armoured is sufficient to cause fear.

[40]The notion of betrayal under trust was obviously very much on James's mind given his mention of a similar phrase in *The True Law* with regard to Ehud and Jael (see *The True Law*, note 67).

[41]The argument here is that disarming would be contrary to the old Scottish tradition of wearing arms; but James's response to the argument from tradition is that if it had been followed, the "old Mass" would still be in use in Scotland. This is yet another example of how James shifts ground to suit his purposes; on the one hand the tradition of divine right to succession is maintained for its political uses, whereas the tradition of wearing firearms is abandoned, also for political purposes.

[42]nothing counterfeit is artful ("rien [de] contrefait [est] fin")

[43]language, the speech of a person or a class of persons, patter

[44]Inkhorn terms refers to a florid Elizabethan prose style, marked by excessive use of Latinate phrasings and diction.

and good grounds, tempering it with gravity, quickness, or merriness, according to the subject and occasion of the time, not taunting
in theology nor alleging[45] and prophaning the Scripture in drinking
purposes,[46] as over many do.

Use also the like form in your gesture, neither looking sillily, like
a stupid pedant,[47] nor unsettledly, with an uncouth morgue,[48] like a
new-come-over cavalier,[49] but let your behaviour be natural, grave,
and according to the fashion of the country. Be not over-sparing in
your courtesies, for that will be imputed to incivility and arrogancy,[50]
nor yet over-prodigal in jouking[51] or nodding at every step, for that
form of being popular becometh better aspiring Absaloms[52] than

---

[45] to cite or quote as an authority

[46] James seems to be referring to those who discuss theology in profane terms
after having had a few drinks.

[47] This bit of advice is particularly striking in terms of James's own reputation
for pedantry.

[48] "uncouth" is used here in the sense of inappropriate or foreign; "morgue"
refers to a haughty demeanor

[49] courtly gentleman. The French version translates "cavalier" as *rodomont* or
braggadoccio (boaster); it seems likely that James is referring more to the haughty
manners of visitors to the notoriously unsophisticated Scottish court.

[50] arrogance

[51] bowing in greeting, but the word "jouk" can also be used in the sense of
evasive movement or action, dodging, eluding, and bending (as in a bow);
Shakespeare's *Richard II* I.iv.23–36 has a description of the kind of behaviour
James is condemning:

Ourself [Richard] and Bushy, [Bagot here and Green,]
Observ'd his [Bolingbroke's] courtship to the common people,
How he did seem to dive into their hearts
With humble and familiar courtesy,
What reverence he did throw away on slaves,
Wooing poor craftsmen with the craft of smiles
And patient underbearing of his fortune,
As 'twere to banish their affects with him.
Off goes his bonnet to an oyster-wench,
A brace of draymen bid God speed him well,
And had the tribute of his supple knee,
With "Thanks, my countrymen, my loving friends,"
As were our England in reversion his,
And he our subjects' next degree in hope.

[52] Absalom was the third of David's sons and is most famous for his attempt to
overthrow his father. He died when his hair became entangled in an oak tree and

lawful kings, framing ever your gesture according to your present actions, looking gravely and with a majesty when ye sit in judgement or give audience to ambassadors, homely when ye are in private with your own servants, merrily when ye are at any pastime or merry discourse, and let your countenance smell of courage and magnanimity when ye are at the wars. And remember (I say over again) to be plain and sensible in your language; for besides that it is the tongue's office to be the messenger of the mind, it may be thought a point of imbecility of spirit in a king to speak obscurely, much more untruly, as if he stood in awe of any in uttering his thoughts.

Remember also, to put a difference betwixt your form of language in reasoning and your pronouncing of sentences, or declarator[53] of your will in judgement, or any other ways in the points of your office. For in the former case, ye must reason pleasantly and patiently, not like a king but like a private man and a scholar; otherwise your impatience of contradiction will be interpreted to be for lack of reason on your part. Where in the points of your office, ye should ripely advise indeed before ye give forth your sentence; but fro[54] it be given forth, the suffering of any contradiction diminisheth the majesty of your authority and maketh the processes endless. The like form would also be observed by all your inferior judges and magistrates.

Now as to your writing, which is nothing else but a form of enregistrate[55] speech, use a plain, short, but stately style both in your proclamations and missives, especially to foreign princes. And if your engine spur you to write any works either in verse or in prose, I cannot but allow you to practice it, but take no longsome works in hand for distracting you from your calling.

Flatter not yourself in your labours, but before they be set forth, let them first be privily censured by some of the best skilled men in that craft that in these works ye meddle with. And because your writs will remain as true pictures of your mind to all posterities, let them be free of all uncomeliness and unhonesty; and according to Horace his counsel, "*Nonumque premantur in annum*,"[56] I mean both your

---

David's general, Joab, took the opportunity to stab him. See 2 Samuel 13–18.

[53]In Scottish law, the action of declarator refers to a form of action in the Court of Session in which something is prayed to be declared judicially, the legal consequences being left to follow as a matter of course.

[54]from the moment; "fra" in the original

[55]placed on a permanent record

[56]See Horace's *Ars Poetica* 388: *nonumque prematur in annum* or "let it [your

verse and your prose, letting first that fury and heat wherewith they were written cool at leisure, and then, as an uncouth[57] judge and censor, revising them over again before they be published: *"quia nescit vox missa reverti."*[58]

If ye would write worthily, choose subjects worthy of you, that be not full of vanity but of virtue, eschewing obscurity and delighting ever to be plain and sensible. And if ye write in verse, remember that it is not the principal part of a poem to rhyme right and flow well with many pretty words; but the chief commendation of a poem is that, when the verse shall be shaken sundry in prose, it shall be found so rich in quick inventions and poetic flowers and in fair and pertinent comparisons as it shall retain the lustre of a poem, although in prose. And I would also advise you to write in your own language, for there is nothing left to be said in Greek and Latin already, and ynew[59] of poor scholars would match you in these languages. And besides that, it best becometh a king to purify and make famous his own tongue, wherein he may go before all his subjects, as it setteth him well to do in all honest and lawful things.

And amongst all unnecessary things that are lawful and expedient, I think exercises of the body[60] most commendable to be used by a young prince, in such honest games or pastimes as may further ability and maintain health. For albeit I grant it to be most requisite for a king to exercise his engine, which surely with idleness will rust and become blunt, yet certainly bodily exercises and games are very commendable, as well for banishing of idleness (the mother of all vice) as for making his body able and durable for travail, which is very necessary for a king. But from this count I debar all rough and violent exercises, as the football,[61] meeter for laming than making

---

parchment or writing] be kept back till the ninth year."

[57] impartial

[58] because an utterance sent forth does not know how to return; see Horace's *Ars Poetica* 390; note that James adds the *"quia."*

[59] sufficient, enough

[60] Craigie notes, using Sir Charles Cornwallis's *The Life and Death of Henry, Prince of Wales* (1641), that Henry was athletic: "In the 7. 8. and 9. years of his age, leaving those childish and idle toys usual to his years, he began to delight in more active and manly exercises, learning to ride, sing, dance, leap, shoot at archery, and in pieces [gradually], to toss his pike ...." (modernized; *Basilikon Doron* 2.264). Cornwallis was Henry's tutor.

[61] See Craigie's note on football, especially in terms of its "extreme violence"

able the users thereof, as likewise such tumbling tricks as only serve for comedians and baladines[62] to win their bread with. But the exercises that I would have you to use (although but moderately, not making a craft of them) are running, leaping, wrestling, fencing, dancing, and playing at the catch or tennis,[63] archery, pall-mall,[64] and suchlike other fair and pleasant field games. And the honourablest and most commendable games that ye can use are on horseback, for it becometh a prince best of any man to be a fair and good horseman. Use, therefore, to ride and daunton great and courageous horses, that I may say of you, as Philip said of great Alexander his son, "*Makedonia ou se chorei.*"[65] And specially use such games on horseback as may teach you to handle your arms thereon, such as the tilt, the ring,[66] and low-riding for handling of your sword.

I cannot omit here the hunting, namely with running hounds, which is the most honourable and noblest sort thereof, for it is a thievish form of hunting to shoot with guns and bows, and greyhound hunting is not so martial a game. But because I would not be thought a partial praiser of this sport,[67] I remit you to Xenophon, an old and famous writer who had no mind of flattering you or me in this purpose and who also setteth down a fair pattern for the education of a young king, under the supposed name of Cyrus.[68]

As for hawking I condemn it not, but I must praise it more sparingly because it neither resembleth the wars so near as hunting doth in making a man hardy and skillfully ridden in all grounds, and

---

(*Basilikon Doron* 2.265).

[62]theatrical dancers, buffoons, ballad-makers or -singers

[63]"Catch" is the Scottish word for tennis.

[64]Pall-mall was a game in which a ball was driven through an iron ring suspended in a long alley.

[65]Plutarch, *Life of Alexander* 6.5. Philip of Macedon said to his son, Alexander, after Alexander had subdued Bucephalus, a previously untamed horse: "My son, seek thee out a kingdom equal to thyself; Macedonia has not room for thee." The reference clearly states James's ambitions for Henry as future king of England.

[66]The tilt involved riding with a lance in order to hit the quintain, a weighted target which revolved and hit the rider if he failed to tilt; the ring involved riding with a spear at a ring suspended from a beam, the object being to carry off the ring in three or fewer attempts.

[67]For a list of references to James's passion for hunting, see Craigie's *Basilikon Doron* 2.267–68.

[68]See Xenophon's *Cyropaedia* 1.2.9–11; 1.3.14; 1.4.5,11; 8.1.38; 1.4.7–9. Xenophon also wrote a hunting treatise entitled *Cynegetica*.

is more uncertain and subject to mischances, and (which is worst of all) is therethrough an extreme stirrer up of passions. But in using either of these games, observe that moderation that ye slip not therewith the hours appointed for your affairs, which ye ought ever precisely to keep, remembering that these games are but ordained for you in enabling you for your office for the which ye are ordained.

And as for sitting house-pastimes, wherewith men by driving time spur a free and fast enough running horse (as the proverb is),[69] although they are not profitable for the exercise either of mind or body, yet can I not utterly condemn them, since they may at times supply the room[70] which being empty would be patent[71] to pernicious idleness, *quia nihil potest esse vacuum.*[72] I will not, therefore, agree with the curiosity of some learned men in our age in forbidding cards, dice, and other suchlike games of hazard, although otherwise surely I reverence them as notable and godly men. For they are deceived therein in founding their argument upon a mistaken ground, which is that the playing at such games is a kind of casting of lot, and therefore unlawful, wherein they deceive themselves. For the casting of lot was used for trial of the truth in any obscure thing that otherwise could not be gotten cleared and therefore was a sort of prophecy, where, by the contrary, no man goeth to any of these plays to clear any obscure truth, but only to gage[73] so much of his own money as he pleaseth upon the hazard of the running of the cards or dice, as well as he would do upon the speed of a horse,[74] or a dog, or any suchlike gaigeour.[75] And so, if they be unlawful, all gaigeours upon uncertainties must likewise be condemned; not that

---

[69] See Morris Palmer Tilley, *A Dictionary of the Proverbs in England in the Sixteenth and Seventeenth Centuries* (Ann Arbor: U of Michigan P, 1950), H638: "To do that which one needs not to do, to spur a free horse." The proverb, "Do not spur a free horse," as cited by Tilley, has a wide range of meanings that add to the ambiguity of this passage.

[70] as in "furnish the space" or "keep the space occupied (with activity)"

[71] open

[72] because nothing can be empty; James is arguing that it is better to engage in some activity than none at all

[73] to wager

[74] James was a patron of horse-racing and held races at Banstead Downs and built several tracks including one at Newmarket; he is also said to have brought Arabian horses to England.

[75] wager or bet

Prince Henry exercising with the pike. Engraving by William Hole
after a drawing by Isaac Oliver. From Michael Drayton's
Poly-Olbion (1613). Reproduced by courtesy of Robert Spencer.

thereby I take the defence of vain carders and dicers that waste their moyen[76] and their time (whereof few consider the preciousness) upon prodigal and continual playing; no, I would rather allow it to be discharged where such corruption cannot be eschewed. But only I cannot condemn you at some times when ye have no other thing ado (as a good king will be seldom) and are weary of reading, or evil-disposed in your person, and when it is foul and stormy weather; then, I say, may ye lawfully play at the cards or tables. For as to dicing, I think it becometh best deboshed soldiers to play at, on the head of their drums, being only ruled by hazard and subject to knavish cogging.[77] And as for the chess, I think it over-fond,[78] because it is over-wise and philosophic a folly; for where all such light plays are ordained to free men's heads for a time from the fashious[79] thoughts on their affairs, it by the contrary filleth and troubleth men's heads with as many fashious toys of the play as before it was filled with thoughts on his affairs.

But in your playing, I would have you to keep three rules: first, or[80] ye play, consider ye do it only for your recreation and resolve to hazard the loss of all that ye play; and next, for that cause play no more than ye care to cast among pages; and last, play always fair play precisely, that ye come not in use of tricking and lying in jest; otherwise, if ye cannot keep these rules, my counsel is that ye all-utterly abstain from these plays. For neither a mad passion for loss[81] nor falsehood used for desire of gain can be called a play.

Now, it is not only lawful but necessary that ye have company meet for everything ye take on hand, as well in your games and exercise as in your grave and earnest affairs. But learn to distinguish time according to the occasion, choosing your company accordingly. Confer not with hunters at your council nor in your council affairs,

---

[76] means of subsistence

[77] cheating; to "cog" dice is to manipulate how they fall

[78] "fond" as in foolish; for a useful note on various opinions regarding chess in the sixteenth century, see Craigie's *Basilikon Doron* 2.271. James sides with those, like Montaigne and Wykeman (the founder of New College, Oxford, in 1379), who thought little of chess, the tradition being that it was almost always played for money, and invariably led to contention. Interestingly, James dislikes chess because it is an overly intellectual "folly."

[79] vexing

[80] if; the "or" may be a misprint of "ere" or "before"

[81] James refers here to the anger caused by losing.

nor dispatch not affairs at hunting or other games. And have the like respect to the seasons of your age, using your sorts of recreation and company therefore, agreeing thereunto. For it becometh best, as kindliest, every age to smell of their own quality, insolence and unlawful things being always eschewed; and not that a colt should draw the plough and an old horse run away with the harrows. But take heed specially that your company for recreation be chosen of honest persons, not defamed or vicious, mixing filthy talk with merriness: "*Corrumpunt bonos mores colloquia prava.*"[82] And chiefly abstain from haunting before your marriage the idle company of dames, which are nothing else but *irritamenta libidinis.*[83] Beware likewise to abuse yourself, in making your sporters your counsellors,[84] and delight not to keep ordinarily in your company comedians or baladines, for the tyrants delighted most in them, glorying to be both authors and actors of comedies and tragedies themselves. Whereupon the answer that the poet Philoxenus disdainfully gave to the tyrant of Syracuse there-anent is now come in a proverb: "*Reduc me in latomias.*"[85] And all the ruse that Nero made of himself when he died was "*Qualis artifex pereo?,*"[86] meaning of his skill in menstrally[87] and playing of tragedies, as indeed his whole life and death was all but one tragedy.

Delight not also to be in your own person a player upon instruments, especially on such as commonly men win their living with, nor yet to be fine of any mechanic craft: "*Leur esprit s'en fuit au bout des doigts,*" saith Du Bartas, whose works, as they are all most worthy to be read by any prince or other good Christian, so would I espe-

---

[82] Evil communications corrupt good manners. See 1 Corinthians 15:33 and also Erasmus's *Adages* I.x.74: *"corrumpunt mores bonos colloquia prava."*

[83] provocations to lust; see Juvenal, *Satires* 11.167, "inritamentum veneris."

[84] James may also mean "councillors"; both words' meanings may be active in this particular usage.

[85] Literally "lead me back to the [stone] quarries." Philoxenus of Cythera, a dithyrambic poet of the fourth century BCE, was placed, by Dionysius the Younger, in the stone quarries at Syracuse for an unknown offence. When Dionysius had Philoxenus brought before him to listen to a poem he had written, Philoxenus is said, at the end of the reading, to have spoken the words, "Return me to the quarries." The incident is mentioned in Diodorus Siculus, *Historiae* 15.6.

[86] From Nero's last speech according to Suetonius in "Nero," *De Vita Caesarum*: "What an artist dies in me."

[87] minstrelsy

cially wish you to be well-versed in them.[88] But spare not sometimes by merry company to be free from importunity, for ye should be ever moved with reason, which is the only quality whereby men differ from beasts, and not with importunity; for the which cause (as also for augmenting your majesty) ye shall not be so facile of access-giving at all times as I have been, and yet not altogether retired or locked up like the kings of Persia, appointing also certain hours for public audience.[89]

---

[88] James's admiration for Du Bartas is evidenced in the two works he translated: *L'Uranie*, printed in *Essayes of a Prentise* (1584), and *Les Furies*, printed in *Poeticall Exercises at Vacant Hours* (1591). Du Bartas had visited Scotland in 1587. James's own reference in the margins regarding this quotation from Du Bartas is wrong. The line occurs in Du Bartas' *Les Colonies*, II Jour de la II Sepmaine, in *Commentaires sur la Sepmaine de la Creation du Monde, de Guillaume de Saluste, Seignieur Du Bartas* (Anvers: Thomas Rualt, 1591), p. 504, l. 579: "Cil du Nord, dont l'esprit s'enfuit au bout des doigts / Qui fait tout ce qu'il veut du metal & du bois ... / Y tient rang d'artisan, & rang d'homme de guerre." Josuah Sylvester's translation of *The Divine Weeks and Works* (1605) renders this passage as "The *Northern*-man, whose wit in's Fingar's settles ... with men of Armes, and Artizans is set" (ll. 605–08). The commentary in the 1591 French edition states that "les Septentrionaux, qui ont l'esprit au bout des doigts, c'est à dire experts & laborieux artisans, inventeurs de l'artillerie, des engins & outils de toutes sortes, representent la vie active & manuelle" (513) [Northerners, who have wit in their fingertips, that is to say experts and hardworking artisans, inventors of the artillery, of weapons of war, and of tools of all kinds, represent the active and manual life]. The point of the passage in Du Bartas is to compare northerners, who represent the active life, with southerners, who represent the contemplative (artistic) life, the people between the two extremes representing the political life ("les peuples d'entre-deux representent la vie politique" [Du Bartas 513]). James seems to be arguing that Henry conserve his wit and resources for more serious (political) matters. Note that Craigie cites an undated letter (probably written shortly after James took leave of Scotland) from James to Henry in which James speaks of wanting to receive a letter from Henry "as well-formed by your mind as drawn by your fingers, for ye may remember that in my book [*Basilikon Doron*] to you I warn you to beware with that kind of wit that may fly out at the end of your fingers" (*Basilikon Doron* 2.40; modernized). Inexplicably, Craigie states that "[t]he king's memory ... must have been playing him a trick on this occasion, as there is nothing like this in Basilicon Doron" (*Basilikon Doron* 2.40).

[89] See Xenophon, *Agesilaus* 9.1: "The Persian king thought his dignity required that he should be seldom seen."

And since my trust is that God hath ordained you for more kingdoms than this (as I have oft already said), press, by the outward behaviour as well of your own person as of your court, in all indifferent things to allure piece and piece[90] the rest of your kingdoms to follow the fashions of that kingdom of yours that ye find most civil, easiest to be ruled, and most obedient to the laws; for these outward and indifferent things will serve greatly for allurements to the people to embrace and follow virtue. But beware of thrawing[91] or constraining them thereto, letting it be brought on with time and at leisure, specially by so mixing through alliance and daily conversation the inhabitants of every kingdom with other as may with time make them to grow and weld all in one, which may easily be done betwixt these two nations, being both but one isle of Britain and already joined in unity of religion and language.[92] So that even as in the times of our ancestors the long wars and many bloody battles betwixt these two countries bred a natural and hereditary hatred in every of them against the other, the uniting and welding of them hereafter in one, by all sort of friendship, commerce, and alliance, will by the contrary produce and maintain a natural and inseparable unity of love amongst them. As we have already (praise be to God) a great experience of the good beginning hereof and of the quenching of the old hate in the hearts of both the people[s],[93] procured by the means of this long and happy amity between the queen my dearest sister[94] and me, which during the whole time of both our reigns hath ever been inviolably observed.

---

[90] one piece or part after another in succession, little by little, gradually

[91] thralling, enslaving

[92] marginal note: "The fruitful effects of the union"; see James's *A Speech in Parliament*, 1603 (*Workes*, 1616), the year in which he came to the English throne: "Hath not God first united these two kingdoms both in language, religion, and similitude of manners? Yea, hath he not made us all in one island, compassed with one sea, and of itself by nature so indivisible as almost those that were borderers themselves on the late borders cannot distinguish, nor know, or discern their own limits?" (488; modernized).

[93] "people" in original

[94] Elizabeth and James were in the habit of referring to each other as sister and brother in their correspondence. A good example of this occurs in a letter Elizabeth wrote to James on July 1, 1598, assuaging James's concerns about the claims made by Valentine Thomas, a border thief who said he had been promised "great rewards" by James to murder Elizabeth. The letter begins "My

And for conclusion of this my whole treatise, remember, my son, by your true and constant depending upon God, to look for a blessing to all your actions in your office; by the outward using thereof to testify the inward uprightness of your heart; and by your behaviour in all indifferent things to set forth the vive image of your virtuous disposition; and in respect of the greatness and weight of your burden, to be patient in hearing, keeping your heart free from preoccupation, ripe in concluding, and constant in your resolution. For better it is to bide at your resolution, although there were some defect in it, than by daily changing to effectuate nothing, taking the pattern thereof from the microcosm of your own body: wherein you have two eyes, signifying great foresight and providence, with a narrow looking in all things; and also two ears, signifying patient hearing, and that of both the parties; but ye have but one tongue, for pronouncing a plain, sensible, and uniform sentence; and but one head and one heart, for keeping a constant and uniform resolution, according to your apprehension; having two hands and two feet with many fingers and toes, for quick execution in employing all instruments meet for effectuating your deliberations.

But forget not to digest ever your passion before ye determine upon anything, since "*ira furor brevis est*";[95] uttering only your anger according to the Apostle's rule, "*irascimini sed ne peccetis*";[96] taking pleasure not only to reward but to advance the good, which is a chief point of a king's glory (but make none over-great,[97] but according as the power of the country may bear); and punishing the evil, but every man according to his own offence, not punishing nor blaming the father for the son nor the

---

Dear Brother" and ends "Your most affectionate sister" (see G. B. Harrison, *The Letters of Queen Elizabeth* 258–59).

[95] Horace, *Epistles* 1.2.62: Anger is a short-lived madness.

[96] Ephesians 4:26: Be ye angry, and sin not.

[97] A bit of advice that James failed to follow with regard to the Duke of Buckingham (George Villiers), his court favourite. For a brief account of James's public treatment of his "favourites," see Goldberg's *James I and the Politics of Literature* 143–46. Goldberg cites Frances Osborne's *Traditional Memoyres* to the effect that James "was seen ... 'kissing them [his favourites] after so lascivious mode in publick, and upon the theatre, as it were of the world' that it 'prompted many to imagine some things done in the tyring-house [dressing room, especially of a theatre], that exceed my expressions'" (143). See also David Bergeron's discussion of James's sexuality in *Royal Family, Royal Lovers* 160–71 and 183–85.

brother for the brother, much less generally to hate a whole race for the fault of one, for *noxa caput sequitur*.[98]

And above all, let the measure of your love to everyone be according to the measure of his virtue, letting your favour to be no longer tied to any than the continuance of his virtuous disposition shall deserve, not admitting the excuse upon a just revenge to procure oversight to an injury. For the first injury is committed against the party; but the party's revenging thereof at his own hand is a wrong committed against you in usurping your office, whom to only the sword belongeth for revenging of all the injuries committed against any of your people.

Thus hoping in the goodness of God that your natural inclination shall have a happy sympathy with these precepts, making the wise man's schoolmaster, which is the example of others, to be your teacher, according to that old verse, *foelix quem faciunt aliena pericula cautum*,[99] eschewing so the over-late repentance by your own experience, which is the schoolmaster of fools, I will for end of all require you, my son, as ever ye think to deserve my fatherly blessing to keep continually before the eyes of your mind the greatness of your charge, making the faithful and due discharge thereof the principal butt ye shoot at in all your actions, counting it ever the principal and all your other actions but as accessories, to be employed as middesses for the furthering of that principal. And being content to let others excel in other things, let it be your chiefest earthly glory to excel in your own craft, according to the worthy counsel and charge of Anchises to his posterity in that sublime and heroical poet wherein also my dicton[100] is included:

Excudent alii spirantia mollius aera,
Credo equidem, vivos ducent de marmore vultus,

---

[98]See W. W. Buckland, *A Textbook of Roman Law from Augustus to Justinian,* rev. Peter Stein, 3rd ed. (Cambridge UP, 1966), 599–602, for more information on noxal liability, "delicts [violations of law] committed by members of the *familia,* i.e. liability either to pay the damages or to hand over the offender" (599–600). The phrase may be loosely translated as "Guilt [liability] follows the source." Or, as in Buckland, "Liability followed the delinquent" (601).

[99]Happy is the man whom external dangers make cautious. For a brief note on this common proverb see *Notes and Queries* 185 (1943), 296.

[100]heraldic device or motto; in this case James is referring to the last line of the passage he cites from the *Aeneid, parcere subjectis, et debellare superbos.*

Orabunt causas melius, cælique meatus
Describent radio, et surgentia sidera dicent:
Tu regere imperio populos, Romane, memento
(Hae tibi erunt artes) pacique imponere morem,
"Parcere subiectis et debellare superbos."[101]

---

[101] Virgil, *Aeneid* 6.847–53 [normalized]. Anchises was a member of the Trojan royal family who, through Venus, became father to Aeneas. The translation of the passage is as follows:

> Others [all those but Romans] will mould in more flowing lines the breathing
> bronze (I do believe), will draw forth living faces from marble, will
> argue more eloquently, will mark the movements of the sky with
> the astronomer's rod and proclaim the rising of the stars. You,
> Roman, remember to rule the peoples by your strength (for these will
> be your arts)—to add law to peace, "To spare the conquered and to
> subdue the proud." [emphasis added]

James refers to his citation of this passage from Virgil in *A Paterne for a Kings inauguration* (*Workes*, 1616): "... he [the king] ought to make it his principal study, next the safety of his soul, to learn how to make himself able to rid and extricate those many knotty difficulties that will occur unto him, according to my admonition to my son Henry in the end of my *Basilikon Doron*, wherein I apply some verses of Virgil to that purpose" (621; modernized).

Glossary

A

ado (n.): action, business

affectate (adj.): affected

agreeance (n.): agreement

all-utterly (adv.): completely, absolutely

allege (v.): to cite or quote as an authority

anent (prep.): concerning

arbitral (adj.): discretionary

archibellous (n.): extreme inciter

arles-penny (n.): money given in confirmation of a bargain

arrogancy (n.): arrogance

astrologian (n.): astronomer

aver (n.): old or worthless horse

avowable (adj.): approvable

aye (adv.): ever

B

backs (n.): forces

baladine (n.): theatrical dancer, buffoon, ballad-maker or -singer

band (n.): that which restrains, binds together, connects, unites

barbar (n.): barbarian

bard (n.): strolling musician (a term of contempt)

bare (adj.): destitute, indigent

begess (adv.): by guess

begouth (v.): began

benefice (n.): ecclesiastical position with income

bewray (v.): to reveal

bishopric (n.): office of a bishop

blanch (n.): rent paid in silver instead of service, labour, or produce

blocker (n.): in bookbinding, the one who embosses the cover with the title

brook (v.): to enjoy, to possess

burgh (n.): town

burreau (n.): executioner

C

catch (n.): tennis

cavalier (n.): courtly gentleman

chalmer (n.): chamber

chancellery (n.): office of the chancellor, the king's chief legal authority

charet (n.): war-chariot

chop (v.): to strike

cog (v.): to cheat

cognition (n.): judicial inquiry to establish the facts in a dispute

commodity (n.): profit, advantage

compear (v.): to appear

conceit (n.): opinion

contemner (n.): despiser, scorner

contrare (v.): to oppose

controlment (n.) restraint

corbie (n.): raven

count-book (n.): account book

countable (adj.): accountable

counterfeit (v.): to imitate

craig (n.): neck

D

dairned (adj.): secret, hidden

daunton (v.): to subdue, to tame, to intimidate

deboshed (adj.): debauched

decern (v.): to pronounce judgement, to delimit

declarator (n.): action in which something is prayed to be declared judicially

decreet (n.): decree

dicton (n.): heraldic device or motto

difficile (adj.): difficult

dilate (v.): to relate, to enlarge upon, to set forth or spread abroad, to inform upon, to amplify, to report

dilator (n): objection or exception which halts legal proceedings until it has been dealt with

dispone (v.): to grant

dite (v.): to compose, to prescribe, to lay down

ditement (n.): composition

dit (v.): to shut up

divers (adj.): sundry, several

divulgating (n.): publishing

doubtsome (adj.): doubtful

dozen (v.): to stupify

E

ear (v.): to plough

economic (adj.): pertaining to the household

eke (v.): to add

else (adv.): elsewhere

endue (v.): to endow

engine (n.): intellect, innate or natural talent, inclination

enregistrate (v.): to place on permanent record

entresse (n.): benefit, interest

ethnic (adj.): heathen

evangel (n.): gospel, scriptural authority

evanish (v.): to fade away slowly

experimented (adj.): experienced

F

faird (v.): to paint (as in to paint the face)

fairding (n.): make-up, painting of the face

fashery (n.): worry

fashious (adj.): vexatious

feckless (adj.): futile, ineffectual

feid (n.): feud

feign (v.): to invent

few (n.): perpetual lease for a fixed rent

forefault (v.): to impose a sentence of forfeiture

forfeiture (n.): punishment or sanction imposed upon individuals by parliament

forsooth (adv.): truly

fro (prep.): from the moment when

freets (n.): superstitions

G

gage (v.): to wager

gaigeour (n.): wager or bet

gar (v.): to cause to be done or happen

governor (n.): tutor

gross (adj.): coarse

gust (n.): taste

H

habitude (n.): disposition, custom, habit

hagbut (n.): early type of portable gun, arquebus

hap (n.): chance

hoard (n.): abandoned or buried treasure

homely (adj.): intimate

howbeit (adv.): nevertheless

I

incommodities (n.): disadvantages

inconvenients (n.): inconveniences

infame (v.): to defame

intromission (n.): dealing

J

janisseries (n.): elite Turkish
soldiers

jouking (v.): to bow in greeting, to
dodge, to elude

K

kindliest (adj.): most natural, most
proper, most fitting

kithe (v.): to make known

L

laird (n.): landed proprietor
equivalent to baron

law-borrows (n.): legal security
required from a person that s/he
will not injure the person,
family, or property of another

leed (n.): language, the speech of a
person or a class of persons,
phraseology, patter

lightly (v.): to disparage, to
underestimate

lippen (v.): to trust

list (v.): to wish

livery (n.): distinctive clothing
worn by members of a company
or servants of a noble household

longsome (adj.): extended

longsomeness (n.): repetitiousness

M

magnanimity (n.): magnificence

maniest (n.): many if not most

mean (adj.): not of high rank

meaned (adj.): lamented

meet (adj.): appropriate

menstrally (n.): minstrelsy

middes (n.): middle part, mean

middesses (n.): means

mignard (adj.): dainty

Momus (n.): mocker

morgue (n.): demeanour

moyen (n.): means of sustenance

N

natural (n.): disposition

O

oblished (adj.): obliged

oppone (v.): to oppose

oppression (n.): wrongful exercise
of authority; unjust treatment of
inferiors

orp (v.): to fret

over-fond (adj.): overly foolish

over-homely (adj.): overly familiar

oversee (v.): to overlook

P

paction (n.): act of making a pact

painful (adj.): painstaking

pall-mall (n.): game in which a ball
is driven through an iron ring
suspended in a long alley

parity (n.): equality and lack of
hierarchy among ministers in
the church

past-master (n.): expert

patent (adj.): open

pay home (v.): to avenge, to pay in
full

peccant (adj.): sinning, offending

pecunial (adj.): pecuniary,
consisting of money

penetrant (adj.): penetrating

pert (adj.): aware

plate-sleeves (n.): thin pieces of
steel woven together onto fabric
and used to armour the sleeves

popple (n.): tares, weeds

practic (n.): practice

preceptor (n.): teacher, book of
instruction

prejudge (v.): to affect prejudicially
or injuriously

prejudged (adj.): prejudiced

preoccupied (adj.): biased

preparative (n.): that which prepares the way for something else

press (v.): to strive

promove (v.): to encourage

provide (v.): to advance to a position of greater importance (used, almost always, in reference to ecclesiastical promotion)

provost (n.): Scottish equivalent of mayor

publickest (adj.): most public

R

rash-heady (adj.): rash-headed

rathest (adv.): most vehemently, most eagerly

reave (v.): to pluck

reciprock (adj.): reciprocal

redact (v.): to reduce

refection (n.): refreshment by food or drink

regality (n.): territorial jurisdiction of a royal nature granted by a king

rehabile (v.): to make legitimate

remeid (n.): remedy

rent (adj.): torn, pulled asunder

responsal (adj.): responsible

rogation (n.): act of submitting a law for acceptance

room (n.): place, position

S

scare at (v.): to be afraid of

searcher (n.): custom house officer appointed to search ships

secrets (n.): coat of mail concealed under one's ordinary apparel

sensyne (adv.): since then

sheriffdom (n.): territory under the jurisdiction of a sheriff

sib (adj.): related by blood

sicker (adj.): secure

skantly (adv.): scarcely

slidderiest (adj.) slipperiest

smoar (v.): to choke

snapper (v.): to trip, to stumble

spouse (v.): to espouse

spunk (n.): spark

square (n.): the instrument by which a carpenter measures the accuracy of his or her work

start-up (n.): up-start

stomached (adj.): offended, angered

strait (adj.): strict

straits (n.): hardships

suit (v.): to sue for

surety (n.): security

surplice (n.): loose garment worn by Catholic and Anglican priests

sustentation (n.): maintenance, divine support

syne (adv.): thereafter

T

tack (n.): leasehold tenure

targe (n.): small shield

textuary (n.): textual, especially biblical, scholar; one who adheres closely to the letter of Scripture

theologue (n.) theologian

theoric (n.): theory

therefor (adv.): for that

thesaurer (n.): treasurer

thrall (v.): to enslave

thraw (v.): to thrall, enslave

thrissel (n.): thistle

throng (adj.): crowded with people

tig (v.): to meddle

timously (adv.): early, opportunely, in good time

tiner (n.): loser

traist (n.): trust

tratler (n.): idle talker

travail (n.): labour, bodily exertion

truchman (n.): interpreter

tuilyiesome (adj.): quarrelsome, contentious

U

uncouth (adj.): foreign,
  inappropriate, impartial
undaunted (adj.): untamed
unmeet (adj.): inappropriate
unrehabiled (adj.): not legitimated
unspeered (adj.): unasked
untimous (adj.): unseasonable,
  premature
use (v.): to tend, to accustom
use (n.): habit, custom

V

vague (v.): to wander
vaik (v.): to become vacant
vent (v): to publish
victuals (n.): livestock and raw
  materials
vive (adj.): life-like
volubility (n.): property of turning
  on an axis

W

wakerife (adj.): vigilant
ward (n.): tenure by military
  service or payment in
  commutation of military service
ware (adj.): wary
waster (n.): one who lives in
  idleness or extravagance
weal (n.): welfare
whiles (adv.): on occasion,
  sometimes
whole (adj.): all of
wrack (n.): ruin, destruction
wrack (v.): to punish
writ (n.): a written work, writing

Y

ynew (n.): sufficient, enough

Publications of the Centre for Reformation and Renaissance Studies

Renaissance and Reformation Texts in Translation:

Lorenzo Valla. *The Profession of the Religious and Selections from The Falsely-Believed and Forged Donation of Constantine.* Trans. O.Z. Pugliese. 2nd ed. (1994), pp. 114

Giovanni Della Casa. *Galateo: A Renaissance Treatise on Manners.* Trans. K. Eisenbichler and K.R. Bartlett. 3rd ed. (1994), pp. 98

Bernardino Ochino. *Seven Dialogues.* Trans. R. Belladonna (1988), pp. 96

Nicholas of Cusa. *The Layman on Wisdom and The Mind.* Trans. M.L. Führer (1989), pp. 112

Andreas Karlstadt, Hieronymous Emser, Johannes Eck. *A Reformation Debate: Karlstadt, Emser, and Eck on Sacred Images.* Trans. B. Mangrum and G. Scavizzi (1991), pp. 115

Whether Secular Government Has the Right to Wield the Sword in Matters of Faith: A Controversy in Nürnberg in 1530. Trans. James M. Estes (1994), pp. 118

Jean Bodin. *On the Demon-Mania of Witches.* Abridged, trans. & ed. R.A. Scott and J.L. Pearl (1995), pp. 219

Tudor and Stuart Texts:

James I. *The True Law of Free Monarchies and Basilikon Doron.* Ed. with an intro. by D. Fischlin and M. Fortier (1996), pp. 181

Occasional Publications:

Register of Sermons Preached at Paul's Cross (1534-1642). Comp. M. MacLure. Revised by P. Pauls and J.C.Boswell (1989), pp. 151

Annotated Catalogue of Early Editions of Erasmus at the Centre for Reformation and Renaissance Studies, Toronto. Comp. J. Glomski and E. Rummel (1994), pp. 153

For additional information, contact:
CRRS Publications, Victoria University, Toronto, Ontario
M5S 1K7, CANADA
(416) 585-4484, fax (416) 585-4591,
e-mail crrs@chass.utoronto.ca